Out of Milk

Out of Milk

Infant Food Insecurity in a Rich Nation

LESLEY FRANK

UBCPress · Vancouver · Toronto

28 27 26 25 24 23 22 21 20 5 4 3 2 1

Printed in Canada on FSC-certified ancient-forest-free paper (100% post-consumer recycled) that is processed chlorine- and acid-free.

Library and Archives Canada Cataloguing in Publication

Title: Out of milk : infant food insecurity in a rich nation / Lesley Frank.
Names: Frank, Lesley, author.
Description: Includes bibliographical references and index.
Identifiers: Canadiana (print) 20200201883 | Canadiana (ebook) 20200201891 | ISBN 9780774862479 (hardcover) | ISBN 9780774862486 (softcover) | ISBN 9780774862493 (PDF) | ISBN 9780774862509 (EPUB) | ISBN 9780774862516 (Kindle)
Subjects: LCSH: Infants—Nutrition—Canada. | LCSH: Breastfeeding—Canada. | LCSH: Food security—Health aspects—Canada.
Classification: LCC RJ216 .F73 2020 | DDC 649/.3—dc23

Canadä

UBC Press gratefully acknowledges the financial support for our publishing program of the Government of Canada (through the Canada Book Fund), the Canada Council for the Arts, and the British Columbia Arts Council.

This book has been published with the help of a grant from the Canadian Federation for the Humanities and Social Sciences, through the Awards to Scholarly Publications Program, using funds provided by the Social Sciences and Humanities Research Council of Canada.

Printed and bound in Canada by Friesens
Set in Zurich, Univers, and Minion by Apex CoVantage, LLC
Copy editor: Camilla Blakeley
Proofreader: Lauren Cross
Indexer: Patti Phillips
Cover designer: Jessica Sullivan

UBC Press
The University of British Columbia
2029 West Mall
Vancouver, BC V6T 1Z2
www.ubcpress.ca

This book is dedicated to Helen Peill (1966–2016). Helen worked as a Canada Prenatal Nutrition Program coordinator and a lactation consultant in the Annapolis Valley of Nova Scotia. She gave her time and support endlessly to mothers in their journey through pregnancy, birthing, feeding, and early parenthood. She was there to celebrate the joys, and there to mitigate the hardships. Full of compassion, void of judgment, deeply understanding, Helen was always there – until she couldn't be any more. She is greatly missed by the mothers. She is greatly missed by me. She was my dearest friend.

Contents

Foreword

I remember a woman in her early twenties who I had seen in my family medicine clinic; she had come to talk about her depression. She was a single mother with an infant and a toddler. Among her many struggles was the fact that she was having trouble affording formula for her infant while on social assistance. At the time I wondered why she hadn't tried to breastfeed longer, given her financial constraints. Now, after reading *Out of Milk*, I would have a much different approach to her food insecurity and, more specifically, her infant's food insecurity.

Despite having studied and worked in public health for over ten years, I made several pages of notes while reading *Out of Milk*. I have been part of many public health initiatives related to breastfeeding or food security, but rarely have I seen specific consideration of infant food security in the way that is described in *Out of Milk*. Dr. Frank has effectively created bridges between individual circumstances and multiple policy areas in a way that is appealing for anyone who cares about ensuring that infants are healthy, which should be all of us. Even more fundamentally, she addresses the breastfeeding paradox: Why are the women who can least afford to buy infant formula the most likely to use it?

Dr. Frank explores this paradox through research rooted in Nova Scotia, filling in much-needed information gaps. Although the content has broad applicability throughout the country and beyond, we often lack local data in Nova Scotia, making it harder to advocate for change. We do know, however, that Nova Scotia has one of the lowest breastfeeding initiation rates in the country. And we also have among the highest poverty rates in the country. Thus, Nova Scotia is unfortunately an ideal place to explore the breastfeeding paradox. The need is highlighted by Nova Scotia's Healthy Eating strategy, which includes clear support for breastfeeding and clear acknowledgment of the impact of poverty on food insecurity – but no specific focus on infants. Even the cover, which is decorated with people of many ages, lacks an infant.

Typically, public health and health care focus on ensuring supports for breastfeeding, usually through one-on-one or group services. *Out of Milk* demonstrates ways in which health providers can better support breastfeeding parents, especially those in challenging financial situations or living in poverty. Although breastfeeding is frequently framed as "free" and "convenient" – which it can be – that is not the reality for everyone. *Out of Milk* is clear on the need to critically assess how public health clinicians and other health care workers may unintentionally fail mothers by not integrating their socio-economic circumstances into advice, even as they and we work toward certain goals, for example, exclusive breastfeeding until six months of age. This book took me out of my comfort zone and compelled me to think about my own practices as a public health and family physician. Increasing breastfeeding is a necessary goal; however, it is essential to prioritize the mother and infant, whatever path is best for them.

Individual situations are important to consider, but *Out of Milk*'s greatest value lies in shifting away from seeing infant feeding solely as a health policy issue to reframing it as a multifaceted societal one. Dr. Frank examines the intersection of neo-liberal policies and infant food security. Lack of housing, decent wages, adequate social assistance, and other systemic barriers make it harder to breastfeed *and* make it harder to afford to formula feed.

These considerations are powerfully emphasized by centring the voices of women, many of whom are single mothers, struggling to fulfill the nutrition needs of their infant and often other children. As I reviewed this book, I paused frequently to reflect on the words of the women who shared their experiences. Dr. Frank's rigorous narrative research was seamlessly woven into the text, leading to recommendations for institutions working with families as well as for policy makers. At a time when media, health workers, and others often dichotomize breastfeeding and formula feeding, the women quoted illustrate how much more complex infant feeding can be. Yet they also illustrate how the complexity is too often imposed by hostile environments in a specifically gendered way. And since poverty disproportionately affects women – especially those who are Indigenous, black, racialized, or part of other systematically marginalized groups – there is even more impetus to right historical and current wrongs to empower mothers and their infants.

The book is highly accessible, unlike many academic resources. I imagine a broad range of readers for this book, from public health workers to clinicians, from community organizers and non-profit staff, from government staff to politicians. It is an essential read for those involved in income and food policy–related efforts, given the lack of explicit attention on infant needs in those areas. And, hopefully, there will be a readership among mothers who find it heartening to see their own experiences reflected in a way that recognizes their struggles, conveys them sensitively, and enables them to be the catalysts for system changes.

The topics addressed by Dr. Frank are of vital importance, given all we know about the importance of the early years for lifelong health and well-being. Infants living in households where their food and income security are assured are much more likely to have positive outcomes such as school success; and long-term, they have fewer chronic diseases and mental health concerns. There is absolutely no reason why any infant in Nova Scotia, or Canada, should be food insecure, whether they obtain their nutrition through breastfeeding or formula or, as many do, a mix of both.

This book is a sober yet forward-looking lesson for all of us working with infants and families or making policy decisions that have repercussions for infants and families: it is our collective responsibility to ensure infant food security. *Out of Milk* provides informative background and concrete steps to make that happen.

Monika Dutt, MD
Public health and family physician
Sydney, Nova Scotia

Acknowledgments

This book has had a long birth. It draws on projects designed to explore food security issues concerning infants and their mothers throughout Canada and community-based organizational responses to infant food need. The research was approved by the University of New Brunswick Research Ethics Board and the Acadia Research Ethics Board.

I wish to acknowledge the mothers who participated in interviews, as well as the policy and program workers who shared their expertise. Thank you to the staff who helped these stories to be heard by providing transportation, child care, and food through the following family resource centres: Chebucto Family Centre, Cape Breton Family Place, Dartmouth Family Resource Centre, Kids Action Program, Kids First Association, Maggie's Place, Mi'kmaq Child Development Centre, and the South Shore Family Resource Association. Many of you I have known for a long time, and meeting you again in the process of working on this book was like seeing old friends.

I also wish to acknowledge my colleagues at the Canadian Association of Food Studies, my sociology colleagues at Acadia University, and my family – all of whom have listened and chatted about this work, offering insights and valuable feedback along the way. I am especially grateful for the insights of the anonymous reviewers who pushed me to reorganize, rethink, recast. Finally, part of this research was supported by the Social Science and Humanities Research Council of Canada.

Out of Milk

Introduction

THE INVISIBILITY OF INFANT FOOD INSECURITY

During the 1990s, I coordinated a prenatal and early infancy program in rural Nova Scotia targeted at families living in low-income circumstances. This program was funded by the Public Health Agency of Canada, and the mandate was to address risks that led to low birth weights and low breastfeeding rates among vulnerable families. The overall goal was to improve health outcomes for Canadian children. I was directly responsible for prenatal and postnatal nutrition-based programming for mothers, which included breastfeeding promotion and support. But in truth these objectives were the long game, often side-tracked by the immediate realities of poverty and food insecurity.

My official tasks were to coordinate monthly food box deliveries, cooking workshops, prenatal and postnatal education, and breastfeeding support. Unofficially, much of my work day and many non-work hours were spent driving families to the food bank, calling churches for food vouchers, and at times securing donated infant formula from wherever I could, including my own family doctor and generous friends. It didn't take long before I shelved the prenatal nutrition assessment tools of the program and left them to gather dust. For food insecure pregnant women, nutrition assessment that made visible a "healthy" pregnancy diet often evoked shame about too many days surviving on toast and tea. For many, feeding themselves and their children was a constant struggle. For me, while my work was supposed to be about improving maternal and infant nutrition, the undermining effect of food insecurity and poverty was sometimes paralyzing.

During this time, I birthed and fed four children of my own. I produced perhaps 2,800 litres of human milk over ten years, yet many of the women I worked with – those who could benefit most from the cost savings of producing their own milk – habitually experienced problems doing so and found themselves facing unaffordable alternatives. Of course, this is precisely the paradox that policymakers were attempting to address through targeted programs such as the one for which my job was designed.

When access to food is compromised, one might expect mothers to breastfeed in order to maximize nourishment both for the infant and, by extension, for the rest of family by freeing resources that would otherwise go to the baby. Breast milk is thought to be a free food and thus, even in a food insecure household, the breastfed infant would have access to reliable, readily available, and affordable nutritious food. Yet I was reminded daily that infant feeding in food insecure homes is far more complex than a casual onlooker might suppose. I understood that my efforts to shape feeding practice had little power to address the poverty that mothers faced when making decisions about infant feeding. But when onlookers asked me why low-income women tended to formula-feed, usually forming judgments about the perceived illogicality, I would pause and mumble a short and inadequate, "It's complicated."

This book is my long answer. It explores, through the experiences of mothers, the *breastfeeding paradox:* why the women who can least afford to buy infant formula are the most likely to use it. It also discusses the opinions of policy workers, community-based program staff, and women themselves about how Canadian policy domains have responded to this paradox, or failed to do so.

My analysis is based on interviews with low-income mothers, a critical review of the formal and informal public policy woven into their stories, and the insights of policy actors and community-based service providers. By examining the everyday social relations of infant feeding under conditions of financial deprivation – and the multiple policy domains that intersect with and shape those experiences – I was able to develop a picture of how household, maternal, and infant food insecurity is experienced, conceptualized, and addressed (or not) in policy and in practice. I have not attempted to provide a detailed policy analysis of infant food insecurity. Rather, through a case study of Nova Scotian mothers living in low-income circumstances, I identify and contextualize where public policy is embodied in the lives of families, report on the current state of the Canadian social safety net for early childhood, and reveal policy tensions concerning infant feeding in food insecure circumstances. Information about the conceptual tools, methodology, organization, and participants involved in the research on which this work is based is found in the Appendix.

My premise is that household food insecurity is a social determinant of infant feeding practice, and that infant feeding (both breastfeeding as a food production system and alternative ways of feeding a baby) represents a special case for consideration when setting food security policy. I argue as well that infant feeding policy needs to consider food security as a necessary condition for optimal infant nutrition.

In high-income countries, food insecurity at either the household or the individual level refers to lack of access to food due to financial constraints, and it encompasses a range of experiences – from anxiety and vulnerability related to food access to consumption of poor-quality food, the need to obtain food by undesirable methods, and various degrees of food deprivation.[1] In Canada, low income has been identified as the strongest predictor of household food insecurity.[2] The outcomes are multidimensional: the material dimension of lack of food or nutritionally inadequate food; the psychological dimension of worry and stress; and the social dimension of societal exclusion in response to deviations from norms related to food.[3]

About 3.2 million people in Canada faced some degree of food insecurity in 2014. Of these, 1 million were children. With 15.4 percent of households experiencing food insecurity in Nova Scotia, where most of the research for this book took place, the province had the highest rate in Canada outside of the territories. Even more alarming, 22 percent of Nova Scotian children were reported to live in food insecure homes. Household food insecurity disproportionately affects households with children, and the risk is especially great for lone-parent families and families receiving state welfare benefits.[4] Food cost and affordability research from across the country provides evidence that neither the minimum wage nor provincial income assistance is high enough to allow households with children to purchase what's needed for a basic nutritious diet, revealing how family food insecurity is rooted in overall political and economic conditions.[5]

How does this affect health? The health-related consequences of food insecurity have been the most frequently reported, with the result that the issue is positioned largely within a public health context in Canada.[6] Canadians who are food insecure are more likely than those who are secure to report their health as merely fair or poor, and more likely to have multiple chronic diseases.[7] For Canadian children, heightened nutritional vulnerability in early childhood can be devastating. We now know that the first 1,000 days from conception to two years is the most crucial time for optimizing growth and development throughout the life course.[8] Hunger in childhood can impair development, affect general health, and increase the odds of chronic health problems for the child at the time and in the future.[9] Less is known about the impact of food insecurity on infant feeding practices, the pathway to infant nutrition, pointing to the crucial need for research in this area. Understanding the breastfeeding paradox requires examination of not only household food insecurity and its outcomes but also many other social constraints surrounding the work of feeding a baby – which is one piece of the overall work of social reproduction.

Social reproduction encompasses the activities, behaviours, responsibilities, and relationships we engage in to ensure human social, emotional, moral, and physical continuation each day and down through generations.[10] Feeding is one of those responsibilities and, like social reproduction more broadly, it is highly gendered in most societies. Feeding work is typically socially constructed as part of the expected social reproduction practice of mothers, and recent Canadian research upholds implicit gender assumptions across ethnocultural and income groups about women's food work within the family.[11] And naturally, the biological imperative of breastfeeding, a component of family food work, makes it impossible to detach from female responsibility. Thus, feeding infants is arguably even more deeply enshrined in ideas about women's natural disposition for feeding work.

Yet there is a discrepancy between a mother's care responsibilities during early maternity – and resulting inability to rely on market forces – and the social welfare programs meant to provide the income security to enable her work of feeding a new infant. The social contract between Canadian governments and Canadian families over the raising of children as a public good has weakened since the 1990s. Neo-liberal social welfare reform has taken the position that care work, including feeding the baby, is a family responsibility, increasingly beyond the sphere of the state.[12] At the same time, fulfilling this responsibility has become more and more challenging economically.

Mothers are held primarily responsible for infant feeding at a time when they often have diminished incomes precisely because of this obligation, and despite pregnancy and early infancy being times of special and costly nutritional needs. Canadian women's access to federal maternity leave has also declined because they have become more likely to have non-standard work arrangements with changing labour market conditions. Additionally, eligibility criteria have been more challenging to meet for women since the mid-90s.[13] If a woman *is* deemed eligible, the federal maternity leave entitlement is just 55 percent of earned income, a statistic with a particularly sharp impact when one considers that women's income in general still falls behind men's.[14] The gender pay gap in Canada is the seventh largest among countries surveyed by the Organisation for Economic Co-operation and Development.[15] Our poorest mothers, those receiving welfare benefits, experience only limited maternity protection from the requirement to seek or engage in employment as a condition of income security entitlements.[16] It is not surprising that gender-based income inequality and increased caring responsibilities mean women have higher poverty rates than men in Canada, and that infants have the highest poverty rate of all Canadian children.[17] Greater poverty in families with young children is rooted in gender inequality, the mismatch between increased care responsibility and decreased earning potential, and inadequate measures of income security to make up the shortfall during early childhood.

The dynamics of family poverty, along with other social constraints, affect decisions about *how* infants are fed.[18] Society sexualizes the breast, impedes public breastfeeding, and poses contradictions between breastfeeding and paid employment.[19] We know that infant feeding trends vary by socio-cultural group, geographical location, and income,[20] and that breastfeeding success is linked to a woman's social position, but researchers have only recently begun to explore how food insecurity shapes the social dimensions of lactation and what and how infants eat in high-income countries.

Historically, breastfeeding has been essential for infant food security, as Gabrielle Palmer describes in *The Politics of Breastfeeding:* "Lactation is the very core of our identity; the process evolved even before gestation and each mammal has evolved, over the millennia, a milk unique to its requirements, its behavior and its environment. It is such a spectacular survival strategy that we call ourselves, after the mammary gland, mammals … animals that suckle their young."[21] Valerie Fildes, a well-known historical scholar of infant feeding, puts it simply: "An infant was breastfed by its mother, or some other woman, or it died."[22]

Today, this is true around the world for formula-fed babies if their access to formula is disrupted by war, natural disaster, or formula contamination or shortage. Although geographic differences exist, infants have an undoubtedly unique experience of food insecurity. Those under a year old have distinctive consumption patterns and limited diets, and their recommended method of food intake relies on lactation typically generated by the mother–infant dyad – a human milk production and distribution system – or access to appropriate breast milk substitutes along with the introduction of solid foods after six months.

I argue that *infant food insecurity* – infant vulnerability with respect to food access, sub-optimal food quality, and inadequate quantity due to household financial constraints – as a social problem, a health and nutrition equity issue, and a public policy focus – suffers from invisibility and poor conceptualization. This is true even though early nutrition conditions are known to be key to the potential of infants to thrive in a host of important areas. While Canadians associate the image of a hungry infant with low-income nations, the risk of food insecurity among Canadian infants needs to be examined. Evidence is mounting of household food insecurity in this country, particularly in households with children,[23] and of a high poverty rate among women and children under one.

In 2005, *Healthy Eating Nova Scotia,* a provincial plan to address nutrition-related health issues, prioritized the promotion of breastfeeding *and* food security.[24] To support the latter goal, the plan outlined an action item to increase the proportion of Nova Scotians with access to nutritious food, which included breast milk for infants. The document did not mention how food insecurity might be implicated in breastfeeding outcomes. This should not surprise us as breastfeeding, and infant feeding more broadly, is usually discussed as a distinct policy issue, far removed from policy debate about food insecurity. Rarely is breastfeeding conceptualized as a food system that may be susceptible to sustainability issues, akin to other food systems.

When infants *are* mentioned in food security documents, whether policy focused or academic, the emphasis is invariably on breastfeeding as a food security strategy. Some argue that breastfeeding represents a sustainable food system in that human milk is readily available, reliable, self-regulating, and environmentally friendly, and thus supports infant food security.[25] Others make the link between breastfeeding and food security because breast milk is a complete food that serves as the major source of nutrition for the more than 140 million infants born annually worldwide.[26] They contend that breastfeeding not only benefits infant health but also helps reduce fertility and increase the time between pregnancies, both of which contribute to food security among infants.

Conversely, breast milk substitutes are associated with high rates of infant mortality and morbidity in the developing world and high morbidity in certain Canadian populations.[27] Infant food insecurity encompasses problems such as the unaffordability of formula, formula contamination and unsafe preparation, environmental costs linked to bottle feeding, the cost to the health care system, and formula shortages due to increased global demand and unregulated trade.[28]

But Canadian public policy has largely ignored infant food insecurity. Canada participated in the Food and Agricultural Organization's 1996 World Food Summit and was a signatory on the resulting *Rome Declaration on World Food Security*.[29] The declaration affirmed food as a human right and committed Canada to action on food security domestically and abroad. Yet the right to food is not established in constitutional agreements in Canada, nor has it been implemented into law. *Canada's Action Plan for Food Security*, a response to the summit, outlined actions centred on the right to food and poverty reduction.[30] Infant feeding was identified as a food security concern and breastfeeding as a key strategy for infant food security particularly, but not only, in low-income countries. No explicit link was made between infant feeding and poverty reduction in Canada.

Subsequent progress reports on the *Action Plan* demonstrate a dilution of food security policy priorities in general. Additionally, action related to

Canadian infants (breastfeeding support to mothers under the Canadian Prenatal Nutrition Program) merited just a single mention in all the progress reports. In 2008, the last progress report marked the end of federal monitoring. Public health experts Catherine Mah, Catherine Hamill, Krista Rondeau, and Lynn McIntyre argue that these reports demonstrate a dwindling national commitment that foreshadowed a government backlash in 2012 against a report by UN Special Rapporteur on the right to food Olivier De Schutter on Canada's food insecurity problem.[31]

In 2017, the Canadian federal government signalled a renewed commitment to address domestic food access through the development of a national food policy. *Everyone at the Table,* Canada's first-ever food policy, was announced in August 2019, in part recognizing that "too many Canadians aren't able to reliably access enough healthy food."[32] While there is much to celebrate with a systems approach to tackling food problems, particularly the recognition of the need for a national school lunch program, the food policy is missing targets on reducing income-based food insecurity and fails to recognize the unique concerns of infant feeding. Furthermore, there is no commitment to a rights-based approach to food access in Canada, a silence consistent with persistent allegations that Canadian governments have ignored domestic food insecurity as a human rights issue.[33] Despite acknowledgment at the federal level that food access is a matter of concern – and some mention in federal, provincial, and international food security policy discussions of the unique concerns of infants – most policy and programming surrounding infant feeding lies within the domain of health policy, where it is not framed as a food security issue. The focus has been on the health benefits of breastfeeding and the ill-health effects of formula. Government resources are aimed at promoting, protecting, and supporting breastfeeding, while regulating the marketing of breast milk substitutes. Apart from the federally funded Canada Prenatal Nutrition Program, designed to support vulnerable mothers in their breastfeeding, little policy addresses the many social and economic factors that undermine breastfeeding as a sustainable food production system in contemporary society – and specifically within food insecure households.[34]

This book is a response to that invisibility. In it, I offer the stories of twenty women with infants, present details of the policies shaping their experiences, and describe the perspectives of a variety of policy and program workers. These stories expose the link between infant feeding and food insecurity due to financial constraint, revealing how the dynamics of gender inequality intersect with those of social class. They illustrate nutrition inequity and the need for food justice to inform policy jurisdictions in Canada and similarly high-income countries. The stories identify infant food insecurity in high-income countries as an urgent social problem. We need to discover how best to address food insecurity as a social determinant of infant feeding, and how best to support early nutrition in our most vulnerable populations.

1

Doing Without

HOUSEHOLD FOOD INSECURITY AND THE FOOD WORK OF MOTHERS

> What if I took your bankcard from you, and your credit card, and your car, and you were living on 210 bucks a month for groceries and your kids have to eat? What are you going to do?
>
> – ANGELA

I suspect some readers know what would happen if they were faced with Angela's predicament. Perhaps you've lived it or know someone who has. Or you might have no experience of such matters, yet you think, "I'm resourceful. I have people I can turn to. I could make do." But how long could you make do? When would your supports run out? And when would the way you live, the way you eat, and the way you feed your children start to change?

The stories in this book tell us about lived experiences of household food insecurity. They reveal the complex relationship between mothering, food work, family dynamics, and food insecurity, and the multiple social relations that shape the interplay of these activities and factors. The families I spoke to differed in terms of composition, size, income sources, and age of children. When asked to describe their monthly household incomes, however, the mothers I spoke with expressed similar feelings of inadequacy, using words such as "broke," "nothing," "poor," "horrible," "not enough," and "sucky." Five women who had once been on income assistance as single mothers considered themselves better off than in the past, describing their income as "adequate" or "okay now" because they were living with an employed male partner, or what one mother termed "a bread winner." Yet four others still considered themselves poor because their partners' wages were low or their employment precarious.

All the women had a child under the age of two and most had more than one preschool-aged child, so they found participating in the workforce challenging, particularly the nine who were parenting on their own. None were in the labour market at the time of the interviews, and only two were receiving or had ever received federal maternity benefits. One of the two, Erica, attributed her poverty to inadequate maternity payments. Other mothers stressed insufficient income assistance or barriers to employment. Their stories also highlighted how various social policies – or the lack of them – contributed to or trapped them in poverty.

The demands of motherhood were key to the women's weak attachment to the labour market. Most aspired to work outside the home when their babies were older, but they saw the barriers as insurmountable for two reasons: lack of affordable and accessible child care; and (for those on income assistance) lack of opportunity to find a job with a living wage. As Anne said, "When you are on assistance you are trapped. You can't get out. You want to get out, but unless you have a good paying job you can't." Kimberly elaborated on this point, explaining how working outside the home when her children were very young only made her life more difficult:

> The kids were with a sitter. One was a baby and I would make bottles, I would pump. I worked at night time. I didn't work too long, a year, then I quit and stayed home because I was working and on welfare at the same time, but they would deduct my paycheque off my welfare cheque. It just complicated my life; there was no benefit for me to work. I wasn't gaining anything.

Mary and Heather still welcomed the prospect of employment, however, regardless of the challenges it posed. Mary couldn't work because of her high-risk pregnancy, but even though having seven children and no car or public transportation had made working very challenging before, she had been far more income secure and had felt better about herself:

> I have experienced working, and I could get a job. The only reason I am not working is because of my health issues in this pregnancy … but when I worked I made $900 every two weeks and I had my child tax and I was able to keep things going good. Making money and doing it on your own, you feel a lot better and you are able to manage, but right now I can't go work.

Rosemary lamented that because she was on income assistance, her mothering work was not considered worthy of exemption from the requirement to seek or secure employment. Nova Scotia, in common with other provinces, restructured its income assistance policies in the 1990s as "workfare" policy, meaning that recipients are required to seek or engage in employment as a condition of entitlement.[1] The Nova Scotia Employment Support and Income Assistance Program stipulates that after a child turns one, mothers must seek and/or find employment or make the necessary steps toward this end.[2] Susan explained this policy: "When the baby turns one year old, social assistance expects you to get a job or go to school if you don't have medical reasons."

A community services policy worker indicated that this significant change to income assistance did not include any clear policy of protection for maternity work, which therefore fell prey to the interpretation of individual offices and policy workers. She noted that this was the case until a policy recommendation was put forward to provide Nova Scotian women on income assistance with maternity protection for one year. The move ensured that mothers were entitled to a reprieve from paid employment (or seeking paid employment) while on welfare, in line with the maternity provisions of federal maternity benefits. The women I interviewed who were on income assistance often referred to this maternity protection as their maternity leave or "my year" with the baby. As these mothers looked ahead to their babies turning one, they worried about the challenges of finding a job that would pay enough to cover housing and food, transportation, and child care.

Because seventeen out of the twenty mothers I interviewed were or had been on income assistance at some point since having children, our discussion of poverty revolved around problems stemming from income assistance policies, whether about rates, eligibility for various entitlements, or more generally how the program was delivered. Income assistance rates were regarded as woefully inadequate in comparison to the real costs of living. One might expect that receiving child support would enhance income security for those who were parenting alone, but four mothers stressed that it did the opposite by leaving them vulnerable to the whims and/or poverty of their former partners.[3] Anne, Mary, Susan, and Sally noted that child support was classified as "other income" to be factored into the overall household financial assets when determining income assistance payments, and was deducted dollar for dollar from welfare entitlements.[4]

For half the families in this study, monthly child tax benefits were the only income available for children's food, because income assistance in Nova Scotia does not provide personal allowances for children. Although child tax benefits are not targeted at food provisioning, in practice they constitute a state-provided children's feeding program for families relying on income assistance – albeit one that is highly compromised by other needs. It was common for mothers to refer to child tax benefits as the "children's food money" and discussions about this income source centred on its importance for this purpose. As Lorraine said, the "assistance part of what I got was not enough" so the child tax benefit "saved" her. The women also very much appreciated the lack of entitlement regulations governing child tax benefits and, in contrast to income assistance, the lack of stigma and surveillance.

Food Insecurity and Feeding the Family

Despite government transfers, the twenty women I interviewed were riddled with anxiety over the routine provision of food for their families. Their stories were consistent with qualitative research in Nova Scotia and Canada that describes household food insecurity as involving a range of experiences, beginning with worry about having enough food and leading to compromises in quality and ultimately quantity of food.[5] Angela remarked, children "constantly eat, constantly, constantly eat. So if it runs out, it runs out. You just can't pick it off a tree." Through the mothers' experiences, we see how various constraints – high workloads, lack of time, the obligation of parents to defer to the needs of their children and, overshadowing all, the material limitations of poverty – shape choices concerning family food consumption.

Mothers' stories of food work – all the tasks associated with budgeting for, acquiring, and preparing food, and feeding their families – were peppered with persistent worry about need surpassing income, as Angela attested:

> Pretty soon we are going to be eating dirt off the ground, cause $3 for a loaf of bread that in my house will last a day and $7 for four litres of milk that last a few days – What the hell? And the price of meat and fruit and vegetables? You can't secure food. What are you supposed to? Hide it? I have done that a few times, hidden lunch food so I would have food to send to school, and then you feel like crap. How am I going to hide food from my kids?

Jessica described her own experience of food deprivation when her baby was only a few months old:

> I worried about running out of food all the time. Every month. Every month. For a while I was spending all my money on trying to keep it [the house] warm for her and I never bought groceries the whole three months that I lived there. People would bring me, like, crackers and a few canned goods.

Multiple financial demands routinely resulted in not having enough money to buy food. Hannah described this monthly predicament in relation to high housing costs:

> We get behind in rent and we always have to play catch up to keep the bills paid. We didn't have enough to pay for this place because the rent is $900 a month with nothing included. It was the only place that we could find that was three bedrooms. We were taking my whole child tax benefit plus $300 from what he was making to try and pay for this place. Then it was not having enough groceries to get through.

Sally and Angela experienced a similar lack of funds for food while living on income assistance:

> I found it very insecure to keep groceries in the house. By the time your cheque comes you barely have any food left in the cupboard so go out and buy … $150 to $200 of groceries for the month. Any fresh fruit, vegetables, milk, bread, you run out of, and then you just have to scrounge until your next cheque because you have to pay this bill, and this bill, and this bill. Then the cycle starts all over again. It was an every month struggle for food when I was on assistance. To plan for a whole month was hard. I would sit down and I would figure out, this many days, this many meals, never having enough to get what I wanted. (Sally)
>
> Some months are ten times worse than other months. Like, some months, things are on sale and you can get a little bit more, but every month I struggle to buy food for my kids, and it is not because I am a bad mother or because I drink. I haven't even bought myself clothes since I had my kids. I just don't. I don't even have a bed; I sleep on the floor. I gave my kids my bed, because their bed is broke. (Angela)

Stories about cutting into the food budget to pay bills were consistent with published research in Canada revealing that food budgets are often compromised because they are more elastic than other budgetary components, such are rent and heat.[6] All the mothers on income assistance who did not have access to subsidized housing had to use part of their monthly child tax payments to cover housing costs. Angela and Margaret described how their children's food budget was compromised in paying for other basic needs:

> I'm on my own with four kids, so I have to pay everything. I have to pay bills, I have to buy my groceries, I have to get diapers, milk, formula, wipes and clothes, and school stuff, and lunch stuff. My rent is $1,350 a month, cause I can't find a place cheaper, and no matter where you go you are not going to find a place any cheaper. I only get $620 from social assistance for rent. That is all they will give you, so I am taking the rest of it out of my family allowance, and then whatever is left is for food, her diapers, and milk, and I can't take my rent [money] and buy food

> and I cannot *not* pay my power to get food. It is just always rent or food, or power or food. It is always something. It drives me insane. (Angela)
>
> They [the Income Assistance program] give me $620 for my rent and $200 for my living. But they take $200 off because I get that much in child maintenance [from the children's father]. But then I get my $1,500 [child tax benefit]. They don't give me enough money to pay my rent, so I am already dipping into my kid's money to pay my rent. It's their money. They [the kids] are paying for it. Last month, we were out of everything and we had a full week that it was a bare minimum. We had one loaf of bread by the time I could go get groceries. The kids were having jam sandwiches. There was no sandwich meat left. I don't even know if we had canned vegetables left. I have never been that bad before. (Margaret)

While these stories show that often food budgets are compromised in order to pay bills, two mothers discussed being more likely to buy food than pay bills, leaving them vulnerable to owing money, being short on rent, or having services disconnected. Beverly said,

> I have heard that people are more likely to dip into their food budget to pay other bills. Me, I'm the opposite. I will take from my cable bill and my rent to make sure we have food in our house because that is a priority to me, as long as we have a roof over our head and food in the house.

Regardless of whether they prioritized buying food or paying bills, however, the mothers confirmed that they could not do both.

Additionally, lack of affordable transportation added to the difficulty of getting enough food for the family. Food acquisition was challenging and costly without the use of a vehicle. Families routinely relied on lifts from relatives and friends or taxis, and then needed to pay for this transportation with money that came directly out of their food budget. Those who had access to public transportation still found acquiring food arduous, especially mothers without child care support:

> I have to take all four kids to the grocery store. I get on the bus to go there, and I usually spend maybe $5 to $10 to get home in a cab, and

> if I don't have the money for a cab, I have to carry it on the bus. You have to have the stroller closed up because it is a hazard, but what are you supposed to do? I can't strap the baby onto my back and carry the groceries all at the same time. You should see it: in the store I have to push the stroller and push the cart, and people are staring at you like you are an idiot. It also limits what you can buy. If I wanted to go buy $200 worth of groceries, I can't because I can't carry it, so I will have to buy $80 worth of groceries and go a couple of days later and buy more, and sometimes you have to go to the convenience store and pay twice as much as you would have to at the grocery store, and then by the time you go back sometimes, you don't have any money left to buy groceries. I don't know anybody with cars, and if you do you have to pay them gas. (Angela)
>
> I don't have a car. I have a friend that takes me or I walk. I take the little ones and I walk down and I fit whatever I can in the stroller, in the bottom of the stroller. I don't take more than I can handle. And sometimes, I'll go down three days in a row to get a grocery order. I'll walk to town and fill up as much as I can and then I'll go back the next day ... It is half an hour away. (Emma)

The mothers did not indicate that their children were or had been chronically hungry because of household food insecurity, but several referred to rationing the quantity of food. Mary explained that her anxiety over her food work was mostly a supply issue, what nutrition scholar Kathy Radimer has termed the psychological dimension of food insecurity.[7] She said, "It is more worry, really. Most of your time is spent worrying about running out." Jean said she thought child hunger was "a very unrecognized problem" and that "people don't think that there's hungry kids out there" but "there definitely is":

> Did you ever go to bed and wonder if your child was getting enough to eat? I am constantly concerned that my kids are getting enough to eat. My one and only worry is, are they getting enough to eat? Even with my oldest one, I am constantly worrying if he is getting enough to eat. I go to bed and I think, did [my child] get enough to eat? He would start crying in the night and I would think that he was hungry.

It was more common, however, for mothers to discuss a qualitative dimension of child food insecurity than actual food deprivation. They articulated a distinction between survival eating (keeping the body free from hunger) and healthy eating (keeping the body healthy). The latter was a desired but unobtainable standard. The comments of several women revealed that the capacity for healthy eating was realized only with a certain degree of what French philosopher and sociologist Pierre Bourdieu termed *distance from necessity*.[8] Bourdieu uses the concept to explain distinctions of taste between social classes. In other words, the social construct of good taste, or what is good or preferable in terms of behaviour, is influenced by how close to actual need the person or group of people is. He argues that those with low social status exercise a taste for necessity based on the function of feeding rather than the pleasure of eating. In the interviews, discussions of food and eating reflected a range of aspirations, usually combining concern that food perform the function of keeping children full and concern that children be "properly" nourished, following sanctioned dietary guidelines. Most mothers believed they fell short of their aspirations to feed their children nutritiously.

Mary, for example, discussed the challenges of creating a healthy meal when living in low-income circumstances: "Look at how many people out there in my situation are feeding their kids chicken nuggets and French fries almost every night because they are cheap … Chicken nuggets are leftover meat from whatever. How healthy is it?" Angela also referred to "bad food," food that was not nutritious but that she could afford:

> I have to feed the kids Kraft Dinner and hotdogs or chicken nuggets, or crap, because that is what is in the house and that is what I can afford. When it is gone, it is gone, and I say you guys have to stop eating so much, and it is awful to tell them that, because they are growing, they are hungry.

A healthy diet was often discussed with reference to the food groups laid out by *Canada's Food Guide*.[9] For example, Lorraine talked about a "balance" of "nutritious foods" and how she strived to provide at least one such meal a day:

> I try to do meals that have some kind of balance and some kind of nutrition in them, but they're not always nutritious and they're not always balanced, but I try. Even if it's one meal of the day, which is not exactly the best, I try to add it [nutritious food] in somewhere else so that at the end of the day we all have had something good.

Anne also talked about food groups and being able to manage only a limited range of fruits and vegetables, with certain vegetables seen as luxury items:[10]

> For lunch I try to make things quick and easy, a can of soup, and for supper, something that has three groups in it. I buy potatoes and carrots. I don't get the luxury of broccoli and cauliflower, and all the other fruit and vegetables I could have. I just have enough to make meals and have food groups.

Sally also referred to *Canada's Food Guide* as guiding her food work since stopping income assistance, in contrast to how she was fed as a child:

> My mom … really didn't care what we ate. Like, she would feed us healthy but if you want a snack, [she'd say] go get a cookie. But I just pretty much want my kids to be healthy, so I just give what's healthy for them. Don't get me wrong; they still have the odd junk and like that. Every kid does. For the most part they have pretty much every food they need in the run of the day and as many servings as per the Canada health guide, and they usually follow that. But being able to afford it is hard, and I couldn't when I was on income assistance.

This qualitative evidence supports food cost research from Nova Scotia showing that certain families receiving provincial income assistance and/or in minimum wage employment cannot afford a basic nutritious diet.[11] Faced with insufficient income, mothers were forced to make compromises such as eating undesirable, cheap, and less nutritious food, highlighting the distance between food preferences and the actual food purchasing context. Buying cheap food was a necessity but clearly not a choice for most of the mothers. Several described the impact of lack of money on their food purchasing patterns, and spoke of feelings of stress and guilt over buying cheap food that was insufficiently nutritious and rarely fresh. Faced with shopping only at the end of the month, when assistance payments arrived, mothers were forced to adopt strategies designed to "keep food in the house," such as buying canned or frozen fruits and vegetables with longer shelf lives, and cutting out more expensive, healthier foods completely:

> Trying to eat healthy is expensive. It's a lot cheaper to go out and buy a whole lot of junk than it is to try to get your fruits and vegetables and your meat. And on a low budget it is very hard, very hard. There was never really any fresh fruits and vegetables when I was on assistance. That never really happened. If there were bananas and certain things on sale maybe, but other than that it was canned vegetables and frozen vegetables and just the cheapest things you can find. It would always make you feel guilty. [My daughter] always had food but whether or not it was healthy for her? It wasn't the necessities she needed, it was, "This is cheap so this is what you are going to eat." But she was never upset about it. She had food and she didn't care, but there was always that guilt in the back of your mind that you wish you could do more. (Sally)
>
> I would get my family allowance and my welfare cheque, but they came so close together it was really hard to plan for a whole month. I would just buy frozen vegetables and canned fruit because I had to plan for a month and fresh produce doesn't keep. I don't think I ever bought fresh vegetables until I got off social services. (Cathy)
>
> One entire paycheque goes to the rent, so that leaves one for everything else and it was really hard to get through the month when buying groceries for an entire month. Of course all your fresh stuff has to be eaten right away or else it's going to go bad, and when you have a two-year-old you need to make sure she is getting healthy food, so I would have to buy a lot of applesauce and stuff that wouldn't go bad but still had some sort of nutrition to it. I feel bad buying these canned fruit and little fruit cups and I will rinse them off with water because I want to make sure there's nothing extra on them. I worry about her getting enough nutritious food, because if we run out of all the fresh stuff, what is she eating? (Lorraine)

A lot of times in the grocery stores, I skip the meat aisle. Can't afford it. Been there, done that. Sometimes, healthy snacks, can't afford them. I've been to that point where you have to make a decision between what you can't afford and what you can have. (Emma)

Emma also mentioned that food marketed to children seemed to be particularly expensive, and though not always that good for them, forced her to make choices that left her feeling guilty:

Anything targeted towards children is – you know – a box of cereal – $8 – peanut butter – cheese strings. It's expensive, maybe a lot of people would feed their children better or be more focused on nutrition if they could really, truly afford things. When you're in the grocery store and you're on a fixed income and you have to make a choice between this and that and they're both good choices but you can't have them both, that's a bad feeling, when you know that this would be good for my children but I can't afford it.

Angela stressed that fruit was a treat in her household, and while her children preferred healthy food, she could afford to feed them only what she considered "crap":

Well, the problem is, and my kids don't understand, maybe I buy $200 worth of food. Well then in four days it is gone, other than the meat that is in the freezer. The problem, they want everybody to eat healthy, but once you buy a bag of apples, that is three or four apples for four kids and it is gone. So next week? Then what? My kids love eating fruits and stuff and they are so expensive, so I go splurge and go buy a bag of oranges and like that is seven bucks and that will last me two days, but if I bought them three bags of chips that would last me almost a week.

For mothers living with the most serious income constraints, quantity was prioritized over quality of food in purchasing decisions, and ensuring full bellies preceded ensuring nutritional quality. Only Beverly stated that the quality of her children's food was more important to her than its quantity: "I find we might not get as much food as someone else because my preference is healthy food and that is more of a priority to me. I would rather get less food but healthy food than get a whole bunch of junk, than [that] my family isn't getting what they need." She and Erica, the most food-secure mothers in the study, both indicated they routinely exercised choice concerning healthy food – but both also admitted that this came at the expense of bill payments and led them to incur debt.

Parental Food Deprivation

Parents faced with insufficient incomes adopted various strategies to maximize food consumption for their children. The most frequent was to alter their own eating practices. Such intra-household variation of food consumption is commonly demonstrated in the household food insecurity literature. An Atlantic Canadian study reported that lone mothers are more likely than children to have food intakes below recommended nutritional levels, because they modify their intake to spare their children from nutritional deprivation.[12] Several qualitative studies have supported the findings of this research.[13]

In the current study, all but two mothers admitted to skipping meals to make food stretch or saving certain food items for their children. They described this practice as commonplace, rational, and the obvious choice considering the circumstances. Mary and Emma, for example, asserted that their children had never been hungry but that *they* went without themselves. Emma said, "We've never been that desperate, but myself, I've went without. Of course I have," and Mary indicated that she could "go a day to two days without eating." Anne talked about "doing without" as routine:

> When my son started eating, like I always try to make sure that I have food for him, ... that he's got what he's got first, and then I come last. It happens a lot, because the money does not go very far when you have to buy diapers and milk and pay power, so I would think as long as I have enough food to keep him fed and stuff then I can do without. I'm not bothered by it.

Similarly, Jessica talked about her long-time habit of not eating as if it were unremarkable, normalizing her deprivation:

> I don't really think about it very much. I usually just get up in the morning and I just do my normal everyday thing looking after [my daughter]. I

> usually don't really think about eating myself till the evening when she is in bed. Then it's like she goes to bed and I sit down and suddenly I am starving and I should eat something now. I do that a lot. It's just a habit, I guess. I've just been used to having, like, no food at all, not being able to afford it. For a long time I lived in a place where there was never any food.

Jean and Lorraine rationalized prioritizing children's food as a parental responsibility for proper development, in contrast to their own survival-based eating. "I know when I'm having lack of food," Jean said, "but my children aren't going to." Lorraine spoke of her daughter being the first in the house to get healthy food, while she and her husband ate whatever they could:

> It doesn't really matter. We're eating because we need to live, so we will eat plain rice or whatever for three meals, but I can't do that with my daughter. She's three, she's growing, she needs healthy stuff, so I try to make sure she's the one that's getting all the healthy stuff, all the fresh fruit and veggies. I'm finished growing; I have a responsibility for this person that can't do anything for herself.

Hannah also noted that she and her partner "would go without first" so that the children didn't have to.

It was also common for parents to "save the good food" for their children, avoiding it even if they were very hungry. Good food in this regard either meant "nutritious" food (most notably milk and fruit) or food the children desired, such as pizza and other food marketed to children. Elaine remarked,

> I just try [to] save most of what I have for [my daughter] so I'll eat the canned beans over a can of ravioli. I don't really like beans, but I'll eat them because I'll save the good stuff for her. I honestly don't eat as much as I should. My kids eat before I do, and my three-year-old eats more than I do. It's hard to keep especially milk in the house because she likes to have chocolate milk and she likes to have cereal and I make, you know like hamburger helper and sometimes it has milk. So milk, and butter, I would say would be the hardest.

Emma talked about how difficult it was to keep milk in the house and indicated that she avoided eating fruit: "Parents go without. You don't use the milk for tea or coffee because you are saving it. You make sure your kids have enough before you eat, even if they want seconds. I won't touch bananas, because that is for [our daughter]." Sarah and Sally also went without fruit in order to save it for their children.

In a few households, parental food deprivation resulted in family mealtime dynamics whereby children rarely ate *with* their parents.[14] Angela and Jessica ate only at night when children were in bed, both indicating not only that they were too busy caring for children to eat throughout the day but also that the habit formed due to household food scarcity. When I asked Angela how she managed to not eat during the day, she replied,

> I'm just so busy, and people look at me and don't believe that I don't eat, cause I gained so much weight from having the kids that I just can't get rid of it. I'll eat if I'm hungry and I'll snack or I'll grab something that I shouldn't be grabbing to eat. If all I have is one frozen pizza, I won't touch it, cause my kids will each eat two pieces. I'll eat leftovers from a month [ago] if I have to cause I'm not going to touch their food ... I'll get all their plates up and ... wait until I see if they want seconds. If they don't then I'll put it in the bowl for later. Usually they come back later and say "I'm hungry," and if I ate it, I would feel like crap because I just ate their food.

When I asked if she ever ate with her children, she answered,

> Well, I'll sit at the table with them. Like, there are four chairs and the baby is in the highchair, and I'll sit at the table while they eat their supper feeding her, but no, I don't get to sit down and eat with them because I'm busy feeding her or there is not enough or whatever. And I'm really cautious about milk, because I can't afford milk. I'm like, "Have a glass of juice. That milk is more for cereal tomorrow. If you drink it now you will have no cereal tomorrow." And how are you going to tell your kids that no, you can't have a glass of milk? Or no, you can't have a second bowl of cereal? Your kids are looking at you like you are doing it on purpose or you are just hateful. My kids have told me, you are so mean.

Mary also commented that she purposely did not sit with her children at the table because she waited to see if there was enough for her:

> After they are done eating then I'll usually eat if there is anything left over. Sometimes I'll pick from their plate if there is food left on it. I'm kind of scared to do that with the babies because there might be some spit-up food. Not very often do I sit at the table. There is not enough seating, for one thing. Maybe at Christmas, but there are not a lot of times when I'm eating at the same time as them, because I'll let them eat first. My kids would never really see me eating. They don't really pay too much attention to it. It is probably something they are used to.

Eating together is an activity of "constructing family" and a platform for the socialization of food norms. Feminist sociologist Marjorie DeVault argues that the structure of family is in fact formed largely through everyday food practice.[15] She discusses the way in which feeding brings individual family members together whom the public world pulls apart. Eating together is at the heart of the social relations whereby we create family and friendship.[16] Margaret agreed that eating together should be a family activity and is important for teaching proper eating practice:

> How are they supposed to know what they are supposed to eat? If you are just feeding them this but don't eat yourself, why should they, eventually? My kids see me eat. I try to eat lunch when they eat lunch. I always eat supper unless I am really busy, but for the most part, when I make a meal, I make it for all of us. I do that.

The goal of the pleasurable "big family meal," however – or even a mundane unhealthy meal, for that matter – was extremely challenging for Heather. She said that the children noticed and worried when she and her husband did not eat, and they would sit at the table and play games to disguise their lack of food intake and ease their children's worry:

> There would be a week at a time that me and my partner would eat nothing and just be going on coffee ... We would feed the kids first and if they didn't eat everything we would take what was left on the plate.

> Even if it was a spoonful it was something and we would do it just so they could see us eating something. They're smart. When you are sitting at the table with your kids and they are all eating, and they look at you and they say, "Mom, how come you are not eating?" They aren't supposed to worry about that. And I don't want to put that worry on them but what do you tell them? So I would say, "Hey, I'm just waiting for you guys." And their dad would say the same thing. They would get done and get up and go away and play and we would finish what they had when they weren't looking. And it breaks your heart. Or sometimes we would make a game of it, and say, "Give me your supper, give me your supper!" Tormenting them. They would play around getting the spoon going to you and you would eat it so to get them playing and they get to see you eat at the same time. But they don't really know that I am eating this because I don't really have anything else.

Heather's story of the dinner table shows how despite her desire to eat with her children, severe parental food deprivation creates social conflict and ruptures food norms.

Turning to Food Charity

As participants in projects run under the Canada Prenatal Nutrition Program (CPNP) umbrella, the mothers I interviewed had some access to food supplementation, although these programs are not uniform across Canada. Some projects don't provide food at all, others provide it only prenatally, and still others both pre- and postnatally. When provided, the offerings vary: home delivery of milk, a carton of eggs a week, or a monthly nutritious food box. Some mothers in this study did not receive food supplementation, and some that did still needed food charity. Mothers turned to food banks the most, although food vouchers from churches, food items from other community organizations, and community dinners were other options. One mother received a donated vegetable box from community-shared agriculture. Some sought extra help from family resource centres (those operating the CPNP project) when all else failed. The staff delivered food themselves or advocated and arranged for food charity sources to make special exceptions when mothers' needs did not align with food banks' service times. Centres were also proactive in designing food projects such as backyard gardening, community gardening, food-sharing cupboards, cooking workshops, and free meals or snacks during all programs.

Eleven of twenty mothers in this study had recently visited a food bank. Of these eleven, eight were single mothers. Five others had used food banks in the past. Only four mothers had never resorted to food charity, all of whom had a working partner. Two of these four sought other means of coping with food shortage, such as adjusting their diets and borrowing money (Lorraine and Margaret), and two indicated that food charity was not needed (Erica and Rosemary).

Problems of Access

The women's stories revealed the inadequacy of food banks when it came to meeting their needs. Some mothers timed their visits to prevent food shortage, and others made regular visits when they were eligible as a necessary component of their long-term household food security work. Heather described several strategies she used when food ran low, from pleading with the food bank for more to finding a different church, and eventually to borrowing money:

> I do go to the food bank quite a bit but they only let me go once a month. And I can't go to any other one because I am within the boundary of this particular one. And they will mark it [your visit] down and if you come before you are allowed they will tell you to go home, saying, "You were already here for this month." In March I went to the food bank and got a couple of things to last a couple of days. I still had three weeks to go before I could go again. So I had to actually call up and explain to them that I had been ... [but] that I have three kids and that I really need help. They told me come in and they would give me a couple of things. It got me through the next couple of days until I could find another option. Like then I could get a food voucher from [a church], and then when that runs out I would have to find someone to lend me $10, $20. That is always my last resort.

Limited hours of operation and rules governing entitlement mean access to food banks is restricted. While food banks in urban areas may open three days a week, rural food banks tend to open for just a few hours a week or every second week. Elaine described how the system worked in her area:

> You can only go to a food bank once a month. There is one around here that is every three months. Also you can go to [one farther away] every three weeks, but you can't go to two food banks that are involved with [the provincial organization]. The reason you can go to [the more distant one] is because they are not involved with [the organization]. But it is all the way downtown and somebody like me who has to take the bus with two kids … and then back with all that stuff, it is too hard, and I don't have the money for a cab to get home. So I stick to the one here, and it's kind of a pain when you can only go like once a month. That would probably be my biggest challenge, because I try not to have to rely on the food bank but I have to, obviously. I do go every month.

Lack of affordable transportation also limits the ability of families to use food banks, regardless of whether they live in rural or urban areas. Angela described the challenge of getting to the downtown food bank that Elaine mentioned, which she called the "best" one because it operated independently and gave more food than most, with fewer restrictions on the frequency of visits:

> It is all the way downtown, so I would have to get on the bus with four kids, and if you are not there at eight o'clock in the morning you won't get in. You will be the last on the list and you will get absolutely nothing, so if you are not there at six o'clock in the morning you shouldn't bother going cause they will line up at the door at six o'clock. It is open three days a week, but you have to get on two buses to get down there and two buses to get home and then figure out a way to carry your stuff with the kids on the bus, so unless I have a drive I can't go there.

Heather also preferred this food bank, but getting there was equally challenging for her:

> That has got to be the best one. Wow. They give you so much stuff it's unbelievable. But I have to find $2.25 to get across the bridge and $2.25

> to get back and I have to fit the food in the stroller. That is if the bus driver will let the stroller on, especially with that much stuff hanging off your stroller with all your kids too. I lost my shame a long time ago because I didn't have a choice. I'm going on the bus and people can stare at me. I don't care. I have to feed my family.

The work of food acquisition from regular sources was daunting for those with little or no access to transportation and several children in tow. Heather's exhaustion, resulting from her combined food work of shopping and charity acquisition, was apparent: "Three out of four weeks you are looking for the food. That's not living."

Denial of Choice, Lack of Quality

Apart from problems of access, food charity denied mothers the ability to make choices, a situation they lamented but accepted as routine. The women cautiously discussed their experiences, implying that they knew they were not supposed to complain or appear ungrateful yet wanting to explain how lack of choice made such charity an ineffective response to food insecurity. Mothers noted that the food they received was rarely what they would have chosen on their own, or what they or their children preferred to eat. As a result, this food sometimes sat in the cupboard and was consumed only in the direst circumstances. One mother even spoke of donating the rejected items during a school food bank drive, joking about whether she would get it again on her next visit to the food bank. Angela told of avoiding food banks for this reason, even though she routinely ran out of food:

> I have used food banks, but I try to not even go to them, cause, and I don't mean anything disrespectful to them, but half the time you don't get anything you can use. There is only one food bank downtown where you can pick what you want ... [At some places] you might get two bags, and half the time the kids won't even touch it. A lot of it just ends up sitting there. Yeah, but sometimes you don't have the choice; sometimes you just do what you have to do. But my kids, they just won't eat certain things.

Hannah said she simply wouldn't eat food from this source: "There are times that the canned food, which is crap food that you get from the food bank, will sit in our cupboard forever. My husband will eat the canned food if he has to. I refuse. I would rather go hungry. It is gross." Heather was similarly repelled by the unfamiliarity of the food she was given, telling of receiving a mysterious item she was unable to identify:

> There was this one time I was at the food bank, I had this thing that was in my bag. I didn't have a clue what it was so I phoned these guys and they told me what it was. It was frozen in this Ziploc bag and they told me it was deer meat. I cooked it up and fed it to my family. I would not eat it. I would not touch it. I didn't tell them because I knew they wouldn't eat it. Most people get to go grocery shopping. We take it or leave it. But what do you do if it is your only resource?

Kimberly discussed the issue in terms of nutrition:

> It wouldn't be the food that we would normally eat. It would be like more bread and pasta, and I always bought fruits and vegetables and I would always try to keep a healthy meal, but when the time came and we had to go to the food bank we would have to eat what they gave us. We would eat it; we would have to. They didn't ask you what you wanted. They just gave you what they gave you.

Mary raised another problem when she recounted a visit to the food bank on the day of her interview, showing me the items she had received and remarking on the difficulty she would have in making a meal from them: boxes of cookies, cans of soup, a box of tea, salad dressing, ketchup, granola bars, generic macaroni and cheese, and a large piece of frozen salami:

> I had to fight for those apples, and the only meat I got was a big frozen hunk of salami, leftover meat by-products, and really you don't even want to think about what makes it up. What was the most healthy thing I got? Processed cheese slices, made of I don't know what, and six eggs, that would be one each, and a carton of milk. Show me the meal that I make out of that other than Kraft Dinner. You end up with all these things you didn't have a plan for; most people have the privilege of deciding what

> they want to make and going to a store to buy it and putting a meal together. We only get that on the 20th [the date the child tax benefit arrives]. For maybe a week and a half you are a little bit happy about the meals you can make.

Jessica also commented on the challenges of preparing a meal from food bank items:

> Mostly they give you canned stuff, I find, and bread. They give us a lot of bread. It's always the same thing: beans and more beans. You wouldn't believe the size of the cans of soup that we got. It was like enough to feed like a family of twenty. It was ridiculous. And then they give you cookies and they give you like a bunch of random granola bars and little juice boxes, but they don't really give you anything nutritional ... There is not really much there to make a meal with. It's a lot of junk food. Like, they give us like chips and granola bars and like, just crackers. It's all non-perishable foods.

Lack of food choice was closely linked to concerns about food quality. The women felt that they were left with only the choice between "bad food" or no food. Bad food was not just undesirable; it was also of poor quality or unsafe, again leading families to reject it or eat it only as a last resort. Kimberly said, "At the food bank you get pretty much the bottom of the barrel. You could play hockey with the bread; there are bent-up cans. I know it is there when you need it, but they could make it more ... not desirable, but maybe more better?" Kimberly's words reveal that she thought it might be too much to ask for food bank food to be appealing, but she cautiously proposed that it could at least be of better quality. Emma, with a surprising and forgiving sense of humour, told of receiving a box of food that had expired decades ago:

> They give you out-of-date products and frozen buns and bread. It's horrible. My daughter and I decided we were going to make a box of Kraft Dinner we got from there and we cooked the noodles and we went to put the package of sauce in and it was golden brown and it was so rancid and I looked at the date and it was 1985. I'm not kidding. I could cry, because I had to explain that to [my daughter], how that could have

> happened. I had already told her that the food bank gave us all this stuff for free and helped us and how positive it was and then we make a box of Kraft Dinner and the date is so horribly expired and it's disgusting and how do you put a positive spin on that after telling her that these places are here to help us? Maybe it got under or on top of something and it just happened to get stuck? I don't think that it was an intentional thing – but it was pretty gruesome. And it just doesn't make you feel good about what it is that you're getting, you know? Everything is in a can or package. I have never seen a vegetable.

Other mothers mentioned similar concerns over dented cans, stale bread, rotten produce, mysterious meats, and goods that had been handled by unknown food bank volunteers.

Socially Just Food Acquisition

While much of the discussion about food charity centred on its problematic nature – barriers to access, denial of choice, poor quality – the women were not devoid of gratitude. Jessica, Emma, and Elaine clearly appreciated the support they received from the food bank. Mary praised the non-judgmental support she received from a church in her area, and Hannah, Heather, Angela, and Elaine all commented positively on the volume of food support certain food banks provided. Yet their feelings were mixed, and were accompanied by highly insightful comments about the barriers that tempered the effectiveness of charity in addressing food insecurity.

A cornerstone of food security is the ability to acquire food in ways that are socially acceptable and just. Beverly and Sally expressed indifference about needing to use food charity: it was doing what you must do as a mother. Beverly asserted, "It is fine with me. I needed it for me and my kids," while Sally said, "At the time I didn't really feel bad about it or low about it, because I needed food and I didn't have money. What else are you going to do?" It was far more common, however, for mothers to express feelings of shame. Sarah talked about her discomfiture:

> There have been times when I went to the food bank for some cans of food, but it's embarrassing, right? I hate it. It sucks, because it's like what

> do you do, right? And, it's like you should be able to have food, there's no reason why we shouldn't have enough. That's how I feel and it's so embarrassing there.

Research in Canada and the United States has shown that coping measures such as food bank usage are often a last resort when other personal management strategies have failed, and that they are both experienced as an indignity and perceived to be an essential community service.[17] Some suggest that they have become institutionalized.[18] The very existence of food banks functions as an important marker of food insecurity and hunger in Canada, and the number of food bank users has served as an indirect measure, although inadequate, of the extent of the problem.[19] Many argue not only that food banks are an inadequate response to food insecurity but that they cause social harm themselves.[20] As Graham Riches, a widely published expert on domestic hunger, writes, "It is highly unlikely that charity alone can adequately feed the hundreds of thousands of hungry Canadians, let alone address their nutritional well-being in other than *ad hoc* and socially unacceptable ways."[21]

Borrowing and Stealing

Apart from (and sometimes simultaneously with) compromising their own diets and/or accessing food charity, the women I interviewed had developed other strategies to cope with food shortage. Elaine accurately captured the variety of outcomes mothers experience in the face of food insecurity when she said, "We have to beg, borrow, and steal, and sometimes it has come down to me stealing food from a grocery store for my child." Borrowing money from either friends or family, on credit, or through the process of pawning was discussed by thirteen of the twenty mothers. Susan commented that she would "get very stressed out about the lack of funds" and "usually ended up having to borrow money from someone before the end of the month." Beverly noted that she had on occasion borrowed money specifically for food, and Anne commented that she "would have to borrow money from someone to do until the next time I have money coming in."

Borrowing money from family members often kept Kimberly, Sally, Cathy, and Lorraine from needing to resort to food charity. Cathy described her situation:

> I have to say that when I was on social services I had more of a challenge to keep milk in the house and you are down to your last few things; you had to borrow money because there was nothing in the house. I would always have to borrow money. I would be borrowing money from my sister. She didn't have kids and I did. Then I would have to owe them my welfare cheque.

Kimberly said, "I had always been independent until I met my fiancé. I had always worked, and when I wasn't working I found ways to get food. I didn't go to extremes cause I had a little bit of family support to help me with food." She noted that it was difficult to ask for help, however, as it took away "your sense of pride," and she stressed that it was important to be careful choosing whom to ask for help "cause then you owe them big time," but she still preferred to borrow money for food than to go to the food bank. Sally, on the other hand, depended on her mother to buy food for her:

> Every month was a struggle for food when I was on assistance. There were a couple times I went to the food bank, but usually I went to my mother and she would buy it for me. I would be like, "I have no money, no food," and then she would usually go and pick me up some groceries to get me through the next two weeks or week and a half until the child allowance came. Every month Mom would get a phone call between the 8th and the 11th and she would know what it was for. She never once complained about it, because she knew the circumstances I was in.

Elaine and Heather talked about how the debt created by borrowing money in this way made the next month's food budget even less sufficient. Elaine elaborated:

> I don't like to borrow money from people, but I did. So when I get my next child tax [benefit], I have almost $400 that I have to pay out to

people and it will be hard to feed myself and my kids and you know it kinda sucks.

Emma and Jessica talked about using credit to buy food. Before Emma declared bankruptcy, she had paid for food and baby items on credit, while Jessica relied on her roommate's use of a credit card:

> I have been desperate enough to use my credit cards, when I had them before my bankruptcy, for milk and diapers. So had I not had the credit cards, I suppose I wouldn't have been able to really afford it. I suppose I would have had to rely on reaching out to family members that I normally wouldn't, or friends, or I would have done whatever I had to do to get it. Well, not "whatever," but you know. (Emma)
>
> My roommate is really helpful. She has a Visa. So she charges it on her card and I usually give her the money back because I hate taking her money, because she needs it like I do, too. But she is really good with the baby, too. She is sixty-nine years old. And she's not on much herself either. She's on very little. She is so helpful. I don't know where I would be. I am eating a lot more, probably because of her. I am a lot more out there now, because of her. But she is really good with helping me out with the baby. If I am out of something, she will get it for me. I always pay her back. (Jessica)

Pawn shops and payday loans were other ways of borrowing. Jessica, Emily, and Heather used pawn shops to secure small loans so they could buy food. Jessica said,

> I actually have done things like pawn my things that I own – my own personal things – just to get money to buy food. So, like, I used to put my iPod in there all the time and they would give me twenty bucks for it and then I would have to pay thirty bucks to get it out. And every week that went by that you don't go back to get it, they charge you an interest of $10. And then if you don't go back after a month or something, then they put it out on the shelf and sell it on you. Yeah, I lost so much stuff

> there that I wish – I regret it. I had a docking station. I had a flat-screen TV. So much stuff. And I could cry. I regret it so much. But I don't regret it because it was for her, but I just wish that I didn't have to go through that.

Jessica also struggled with payday loans, as did Kimberly. Jessica had defaulted on a loan and had to change her phone number and bank account in order to hide from creditors:

> Oh my god, oh my god, oh my god. I [took out a payday loan]. And when you're on social assistance, they will only allow you up to a $100 loan, right? I could not afford to pay them back. I still haven't paid them back. I probably owe about $700 or more by now. They harassed me and harassed me and harassed until eternity, until I changed my number. I should never have done it. I live under the poverty line; how the hell do I pay it back?

Kimberly and her husband were in a vicious circle of repeatedly taking out high-interest payday loans to get through the month:

> There is a no-win situation there. You pay it the next payday you get, or you can make payments in between. We have to get a loan to pay off the loan. I have been on loans now for four years and I would like to get out. And you try to get out and they say, well you can wean yourself off. And you have to be careful with payday loans if you are on social assistance. If they find out you borrowed, they can actually dock you, cause that is another income. No win, it is crazy, and then they wonder why there are starving kids.

Five mothers talked about stealing food. Hannah, Mary, Elaine, and Angela provided details on how it was possible to steal bags of groceries and larger items from grocery stores with the use of recycled bags and store "purchased" stickers. Mary's cousin regularly stole food that she gave to Mary and once, when Mary herself stole, she was caught: "I will admit that I stole once from Walmart and I got caught. I had to do it for the kids. I had to do an adult provision something-or-other, and I had to pay $75 to the [Children's Hospital]." Elaine talked about knowing people who stole "two or three times a month":

> It could be food, meat; it could be baby food like the jars; it could be formula; it could be diapers, wipes, anything that's supported around feeding children, you know – not just themselves, but children. It's mostly children, you know, and that sucks. They didn't have to be brought into poverty, and this is what we are living in. We're living in poverty because of why?

For Heather and her husband, stealing was the last resort for feeding their children when all other options were depleted:

> If I am going to do that to feed him [the baby], then I am going to do it. And my partner, if he is at work and he is packing up a box and he sees $20 lying on the floor he's going to put it in his pocket instead of putting it in the box, because he knows that he has to feed his boy. And the boss finds out they are out $20, and then they are all up shit's creek because he doesn't want to admit he has to feed his boy. But we did what we had to do. We might have only done it a handful of times but we did it. I am not proud of it but we did it. My kids are still alive.

Angela's experiences with food charity had been so frustrating, unhelpful, and degrading that she preferred stealing:

> You have to beg and plead so that is why, if it comes down to it, I will do whatever I have to do to get money for my kids. If I have to choose between begging and stealing, I'll steal, because you don't feel so degraded, and if you get caught, well, you get caught. At least I didn't have to beg.

Feeding and Motherhood

Much has been written about food work as symbolic of good mothering, and about the "proper" family meal as an indicator of family well-being.[22] The current study also revealed the centrality of food in the daily work of mothers and in family routines, illustrating that mothers took pride in their feeding work when they had the resources they needed. At the same time, their experiences illustrate how food insecurity can constrain food work and shape the dietary intake and nutritional status of families living in poverty.

I asked the women to describe the significance of food in their households. Sally responded, "I have five people in the house to feed, so food is important." Lorraine described food as the thing that kept the family "nourished, full, and happy and healthy." The task of feeding children was the primary activity of their mothering, and acquiring food, preparing food, feeding, and cleaning up afterward consumed a large proportion of each mother's time. The interviews also revealed acutely ambivalent attitudes toward food and feeding. Food had the power to bring great pleasure as well as great anxiety and frustration, depending on how secure a mother felt about her capacity to keep food in the house that was desirable to family members. A full fridge and a cupboard with a variety of food symbolized security, the opposite despair. Jean stated,

> Some people describe shopping as one of those joyful things to do. Me, it's grocery shopping. Well, I guess not really the process of grocery shopping, [but] I enjoy going to the fridge and seeing all kinds of different things to pick from. When I open the fridge and see stuff there, I feel awesome, just the variety of different foods and knowing that I have all kinds of different foods.

As food work constituted so much of the daily work of mothers, the capacity to perform that work well symbolized accomplished mothering for some. Hannah described the pleasure she experienced in cooking a "big meal" and being able to share meals with others outside her nuclear family:

> I like cooking meals for people, which makes our budget even tighter. I'm like "Let's have all these people over and I'll make the food." Can't afford to do it, but I like to. I love cooking for people. I enjoy it. I like to be able to sit down and watch people enjoy a meal. [My husband] enjoys the fact that I cook because his mom only ever made things like macaroni noodles with tomato soup on them and that would be like their meal for

> a month on end, or it would be like a Hamburger Helper. And I'm more like, okay, let's have some haddock and broccoli and carrots or let's have pork roast done with mushroom soup and some broccoli and rice – just big meals.

Mary, who had five children to feed, also mentioned the concept of the big meal, which she too equated with "goodness," in contrast to meals that used prepared food products:

> I have to make things like Hamburger Helper, which is a bad meal, but I guess you are still getting all your stuff in it. But the kids like big meals, like potatoes and pork chops, meatloaf and another vegetable, and that would be like a big meal, but I can't make them very often and I feel bad. If I was to buy a roast, like one you would buy for your whole family, I would have to cut it in two and get two meals out of it, so there are no times when people get seconds. They don't get that opportunity.[23]

For both mothers, the big meal did not mean large quantities of food for each person but rather the ability to feed many people "properly," meaning with non-processed food items that included meat, potatoes, and vegetables.

While producing a "good" meal brought pleasure and feelings of accomplished mothering, stories of daily food work were far more likely to focus on the non-pleasurable, mundane, and frustrating work of producing the routine "simple" meal. This was consistent with a study in the United States revealing how food work in low- and middle-income families is often perceived as demanding and guilt ridden, when constraints limit the ability to perform food work in ways that match the ideals of the proper family meal.[24] Elaine described the ambivalence she felt about food, and how this manifested itself in her feelings about herself as a mother:

> When it comes down to it, I'm in emergency situations quite a bit. When I'm in a good place, like you know my cupboards are full, my fridge is full, and my freezer is full, I'm feeling pretty good and you know, it makes me happy, like I'm doing a good job as a mother, but when my fridge

> starts getting empty, and my milk starts getting low and I'm running out of things that [my daughter] will eat it, doesn't make me feel very good as a person or as a mother. (Elaine)

When mothers fell short of the ideal of properly providing for children, they experienced guilt, shame, and despair. Heather talked about feeling suicidal when she believed she could not provide:

> Sometimes honestly I just wanted to jump off the bridge or have someone hopefully stab me because what kind of mom or dad can't provide for their child? You feel like a piece of poop. I brought this child into the world and I can't take care of it. I don't know. You get through it. They keep you going and you always manage to find a way somehow. The kids keep you going.

Cathy said, "It doesn't make you feel good [when you run out of food] and you think, 'How am I going to feed my kids for the month?' It does stress you out. It was hard." Susan commented that she now avoided going to the food bank because of the way it made her feel: "I used to go, when I had my first son, quite often, but now I don't go at all. I don't really, like I don't like going, because it made me feel like I couldn't afford to look after him properly."

The issue was not limited to self-criticism. Jessica frequently had to call her income assistance worker when she ran out of money for food, but she soon learned that asking for help led to judgment about her ability to care for her child:

> I was calling almost every month for a purchase order for food and [the income assistance worker] started saying, "What are you doing with your money?" and she started getting really nasty and I kept trying to tell her, "Well I am living in this house which has no heat and I am trying to put oil in it every week." But [she] tries to make it look like you are not taking care of your baby and stuff.[25]

Emma, who was working extremely hard raising four children on her own, was accused of sitting home and doing nothing all day. She knew this wasn't true and tried to be strong, but the pressure of the work and the criticisms still deeply affected her:

> I have my bad days. I have times when, you know, I cry all day, but then I don't let it get me, you know? I have to get it out and I have to find a solution for whatever the problem is because I am very focused. I have to be. It's not a choice. I can't slack off. I can't not be responsible – I have to do right by these children. It's my job. Then people will say to you that you're sitting home and you're doing nothing.

Elaine, Mary, Angela, and Emily all talked about fearing that child protection services (CPS) would take their children from them because of their struggles to provide.[26] Mary had a history with CPS: one daughter was already living in permanent foster care and her other children had once been temporarily removed. Emily's child was apprehended at birth and remained in foster care until she was twelve months old. Angela and Elaine argued against claims that they were "bad mothers":

> Every month I struggle to buy food for my kids, and it is not because I am a bad mother. People look at you and they judge you. I have felt guilty or ashamed having to ask anybody for help, but if it comes down to it, I would come here [the family resource centre] and ask, but then I worry, are they going to call Children's Aid on me because I don't have enough money to feed my kids and I'm here begging for help? That is another problem too, like if you cannot afford to feed your kids or you come to too many people looking for help, they can take your kids from you, no matter how well you are trying to do it. But I say, well then give me more money to do it then. You are going to take my kids from me because I don't have no money? All my money goes to my kids, every cent I get. (Angela)
>
> I have had people in the last year tell me that I am not a good mother, I do not provide for my children, that CPS is going to come to my house and that I better have a clean house. I've had people tell me that my kids are going to get taken away from me because I don't care for my children ... I know I am doing the best job I can with the resources that I have, and for somebody to tell me that I'm not doing a good job? They

> can go to hell ... I know that I am not the best mother because I do have my breakdowns, but I am a good mother. (Elaine)

Being food insecure while having the responsibility to feed children left mothers feeling that they were set apart from people who acquired food through regular channels, buying and eating what they wanted. Mary indicated that "mothers like us" could participate only occasionally in the normal routines of food work and food consumption. Heather remarked that people in poverty had to "take it or leave it" when it came to relying on charity, while others had the privilege of grocery shopping and choice. These feelings of social exclusion illustrate well Kathy Radimer's conceptualization of the social outcomes of food insecurity that are manifested in deviations from social food norms.[27]

What about the Babies?

These stories of family poverty, household food insecurity, maternal food work, and the social policy dynamics that help or hinder that work bring to light the need to examine infant feeding as a component of the overall financial constraints on the feeding work of mothers. They also suggest that food practices shaped by poverty and food insecurity may differ by gender, age, and social position within the family.

Thus, infants' experience of food insecurity differs from that of other household members. The social status of infancy, and the fact that babies are (or are not) fed through the bodies of their mothers, is an element of the overall gendered work of feeding the whole family within food insecure conditions, at a time in life when material resources are limited by intensive caregiving responsibilities. The stories in this chapter reveal a great deal about the environments within which infants are fed, illuminating the challenges of food access and food quality in general and mothers' food access in particular. The following chapters focus on how various infant feeding practices are shaped by the social condition of household and maternal food insecurity. They develop a typology of infant food insecurity that demonstrates how infant feeding can shape the social condition of household food insecurity and, even more significant, how the social condition of household and maternal food insecurity shapes infant feeding practices.[28]

2

When Breastfeeding Works

A FOOD SECURITY MEASURE

> I knew that there was no money and I wasn't going to be able to afford formula if I absolutely needed it. I had so many people say, "Well, if you don't have enough milk you're going to have to buy formula," and I was like, "I have to have enough milk. I need to produce enough milk. I have to."
>
> – HANNAH

When access to food is compromised, one might expect mothers to breastfeed in order to maximize food for the infant and thus for the whole family through the savings on food purchases. The women I interviewed did indeed express this logic when discussing their motivations about and experiences of breastfeeding. Although breastfeeding was assigned multiple meanings, "not just about food," they were quick to highlight the food production benefits. Mothers described how successful breastfeeding had the potential to provide food security for their babies. They discussed breastfeeding in terms of food production through references to *milk supply, milk production, drying up,* and *pumping.*

Breastfeeding, unlike other food production systems, simultaneously involves food production, feeding, and food consumption. The production occurs as a social relationship and a biological system of supply and demand: one that requires a *lactator* (producer) and an equally important *suckler* (eater). As a component of food work, breastfeeding thus holds a biological imperative that positions mothers' work, and the responsibility for that work, as central to infant food security.

The women described complex feeding histories, revealing the difficulty of classifying feeding type. While some executed a planned strategy for feeding their babies, most experienced shifts in practice across children and/or combined several feeding strategies at any one time based on physiological issues and/or changes in their family situation. It was therefore difficult to classify mothers as either breastfeeders or non-breastfeeders. Also, to understand infant feeding practice we need to pay attention not only to *food sources* but also to *modes of feeding*. The distinction between breastfeeding and bottle feeding – with respect to feeding with human milk or with breast milk substitutes – was somewhat blurry. Even more complex was the disjuncture between mothers' stated beliefs about optimal infant feeding, their feeding intentions, and their actual infant feeding practice.

Beliefs, Intentions, and Practices

Regardless of feeding outcomes, it was clear that pervasive messages about the benefits of breastfeeding had infiltrated the consciousness of all the mothers, as they all, to varying degrees, affirmed that breastfeeding was "the best way to feed babies." Yet these beliefs were often misaligned with intention or preference, as reflected in statements such as "I know breastfeeding is the best thing for babies, but ...," or "I wanted to breastfeed my children but ..." Mothers qualified their acceptance of the "breast is best" discourse with reasons why they did not intend to breastfeed or did not adopt or sustain the practice.

Three mothers had planned to feed their babies formula from the onset. Four others had expected to mix breastfeeding (or bottle feeding with breast milk) with formula use, or had shifted their feeding intentions from one baby to the next, indicating that intention and practice were contingent on social circumstances. Thirteen out of the twenty women had intended to breastfeed all their children but had either done so for shorter periods than they originally intended or had failed to establish breastfeeding.

Four mothers had met the Health Canada recommendation to breastfeed exclusively for at least the first six months for all their children. Beverly had breastfed two children for eighteen months (introducing solid foods at six months) and was exclusively breastfeeding her six-month-old. Hannah had breastfed two children to just under two years old, introducing solid foods at six months, and was exclusively breastfeeding the three-month-old. Kimberly breastfed one of her children for two years and her other two children for nine months. Finally, Sarah breastfed her first child for twelve months and was breastfeeding her twenty-two-month-old.

Susan, Jean, Sarah, and Rosemary had variable feeding intentions. Susan and Jean both ascribed this to circumstances. Susan did not breastfeed her second child, explaining that because her first and second children were close in age she didn't think she would have the time. Jean during pregnancy had planned to use a mixed feeding approach with her twins, indicating she wanted to use more than one method because she was concerned about the quantity of milk she could produce: "I was planning to breastfeed and formula-feed them. I didn't know whether I would be able to produce enough. But I had them premature. He was in the hospital for the first two months. And in the stress I dried up." With her next baby, Jean again thought she might mix breast milk and formula because that was the approach she was used to. In fact, she wound up breastfeeding exclusively because the child had a negative reaction to formula:

> And my second baby, I wasn't quite sure if I wanted to breastfeed or formula-feed. But I wanted to breast-pump and formula-feed so I wouldn't be tied down; but I'm breastfeeding full time because I think he is allergic to whey protein in formula. I've tried to switch him over to formula but it comes out the other end. Yes, and because that is more healthy, they say. It is more natural so it would be more healthy and it's better for allergies, and allergies run in the family.

Sarah breastfed her first child and was adamant that she did not want to do so again, but like Jean, in the end she breastfed her second child. These stories show the difference between stated beliefs about optimal feeding, intentions, and actual feeding practices.

Collectively the mothers had sixty-one children, and many had more than one child under the age of two. Some breastfed the baby but depended on formula to feed the toddler, or they breastfed one child but not the next, or vice versa. Therefore my conversations with them about feeding included stories about feeding all their children, not only the youngest. Many of the mothers experienced both breastfeeding and bottle feeding, and bottle feeding included bottle feeding with breast milk (and in one instance another's breast milk), commercial infant formulas, and occasionally other liquids.

All twenty women put at least one of their babies to the breast in an effort to breastfeed, and almost all the children experienced at least this attempt. Only about a third of the children were exclusively breastfed to six months, however, while another third were either exclusively or mostly fed formula, and 85 percent were fed commercial infant formula at some point in their first year. Thus, while the breastfeeding initiation rate was high, so too was the rate of formula use. Formula was evidently an important component of the diets of these babies. Also, 15 percent were fed formula alongside breast milk up to as old as six months. Breast milk and breast-milk substitutes of many types were the food items most frequently used within the first year of feeding, but some infants were occasionally fed other liquids in emergencies: juice, powdered cow's milk, fresh cow's milk, and canned cow's milk. Solid foods were introduced as early as four months in some cases.

A Sustainable, Affordable, and Healthy Food System

The mothers largely justified their belief that breastfeeding (or at least breast milk) was optimal for babies by referring to concepts of health and household economics in vague statements about breast milk being "healthier" or "better" than formula. For example, Margaret implied that anything other than breast milk was "junk food": "I wanted them to eat extremely healthy, not junk or processed junk. I wanted to breastfeed them all, but it didn't work out that well." Beverly stated that she based her infant feeding decisions on "what is best for the baby," saying, "In a different world, if formula was better, then I would have chosen formula no matter how much it would have cost and I would have worked with that." Both she and Emma mentioned specific nutritional qualities of breast milk and associated health outcomes:

> I had planned and succeeded to breastfeed all of my babies exclusively, and they never had any formula. I did a lot of research into it. I wanted

> to breastfeed and to me that was my only option. I know there are well over a hundred things in breast milk that formula can never have: immunities, the things the babies get from their moms like colostrum. (Beverly)
>
> I just knew that the breast was the best because of all the nutrients and the brain development and the DHA. I just said to myself, wow, then that's what I'm going to do then. It's what's best for my baby. It's going to make her smarter and less gassy and less ear infections and it is better. (Emma)

Lorraine also highlighted attributes of breast milk:

> Well I planned to breastfeed them both. I do think that breast is best, and I think that it's free, there is no risk of cross-contamination, it's there, it's ready, it's the right amount, it's the perfect food, it adapts to your baby needs, so if you have a preemie your milk is different than if you have a full-term baby. As your baby gets older your milk matures. It's amazing.

While health justification was common to all, for this group of mothers the cost of formula was also a motivation, indicating that household food insecurity may be a predictor of breastfeeding initiation. Thirteen mothers noted the economic benefit of breastfeeding to the household. The four who met the exclusive breastfeeding recommendation for all their children, along with the eight who exclusively breastfed at least one of their children, considered their infants food secure in terms of survival, food safety (lack of contamination), quality (a healthy food source ideally adapted for the infant's developmental stage), and access (readily available and affordable supply).

Although anxiety about household food insecurity was persistent, at least it was suspended with respect to the baby in the family. For example, Emma declared, "It's amazing to think that I sustain her life. It's powerful. It's awesome to think that she's alive because of my breast milk." Erica said, "You know your baby is never going to go hungry. You don't have to worry about where you are going to get food and where the money is going to come from." Similarly, Lorraine discussed the suspension of worry that came with breastfeeding:

> It's a big comfort knowing that my son is going to have milk when he needs it any time of day or night, like I don't have to do anything, it's there. And with my daughter, I was so stressed out just thinking how we only have $20 in the bank and it's $30 for formula, we have one can left and no money. Back then I would think, why didn't I just stick with the breastfeeding? Why didn't I just work harder? A hundred dollars a month I would have saved for those nine months she was on formula. But now with my son, I'm so much more relaxed about everything knowing that he's not going to be hungry.

Jean also indicated that she did not have to be concerned even when she was away from her baby, as she and her friend had on occasion used their own frozen breast milk to feed the other's baby when providing child care.

Several mothers described breastfeeding as a strategy to address household food insecurity. "I wanted to breastfeed," Mary said, "because have you seen the price of formula? Mainly the cost of it. Most people are 'Oh, it is so healthy for them,' and I'm like, 'Yeah, but for me, I'm using that money to buy all the other stuff for the other kids too.' It is expensive to buy formula; it really is." Hannah viewed breastfeeding as the only affordable option: "If I hadn't been so determined, I would have given up. If I had thought that I could afford formula, I may have given up." Similarly, despite not wanting to breastfeed her second baby, Sarah did so because she worried about food shortages within the family:

> With my first child, I was totally set on nursing. It was the most natural thing to do; like, if it's there, use it. Even before I got pregnant, I always thought that I would nurse. And my second child was totally unsuspected, so I said I am not nursing ever again … but I started thinking that I won't be able to afford formula. And it's always there and I would be scared: What if I ran out? What if I didn't have enough formula to go the whole month? Then what? So I decided I was only going to nurse her at night time so I wouldn't have to get up in the middle of the night, and then I just said, no, I will strictly breastfeed her.

Lorraine commented on breast milk being "free," adding, "Why would you pay $100 a month to feed your baby something that you are making, that is an imitation of something that you have for free?"

While a few mothers (those with more moderate food insecurity and a working partner) mentioned only health as a reason to breastfeed, several others discussed economic and health reasons in tandem. Sally, Heather, Anne, and Erica offered this dual explanation. Sally, for example, commented, "Well, I knew I was going to breastfeed because that definitely cuts out a huge cost and it's healthy for them. The two were pretty much head to head: the cost and what is good for them."

Although mothers believed their infants were food secure as long as they were breastfed, they noted that the practice did not translate into more money for other things. The value and scarcity of breast milk was acknowledged – some stated that it was "like gold" – but its economic value was contested. As Beverly explained, there is little option to *save* food money when there is little money to begin with: "I wouldn't say there is more money for food, 'cause buying formula was never put into the equation. It is not like we said, 'Oh well, formula is going to be a hundred bucks a month' or whatever, so it is not that we have an extra hundred for groceries. It was never there to begin with."

Other reasons for believing that breastfeeding was the better option focused on the feeding act. A few women mentioned the convenience of breastfeeding. Heather said, "I could go out and just take the baby with me and all I would have to do is take diapers," implying that the work of formula feeding was more onerous. Emma combined convenience with food quality and economic justifications for preferring breastfeeding: "I wanted to breastfeed for the economical value of it, of course, and also for the health benefits, and also for the convenience. There's a whole spectrum of different reasons why, not just one. You just know that it's best and it's convenient and cheaper, and all those things combined."

Others referred to the notion of breast milk and breastfeeding being "natural food" and "traditional food practice." As Sarah stated, "It was the most natural thing to do; like, if it's there, use it." In these cases, mothers did not consider breastfeeding to require much deliberation, as it was part of an already established sense of feeding and food practice within their immediate social groups. For example, Erica suggested that the fact that she and her siblings were breastfed probably contributed to her desire to do the same. Hannah described the practice as part of her family tradition:

> I was always going to breastfeed. It was never a question to me. It was just that's how babies are fed and so I was automatically going to do it. I was determined that this was what I was going to do and I was not going to give my baby formula. It wasn't that I thought formula was bad or that breastfeeding was better. It was just *what I knew, what I do*. I grew up with my mom talking about breastfeeding and how she breastfed all of us and my aunt had breastfed. I'd always seen people bottle-feed, but it was never even a thought to do that. If I had done anything else [other than breastfeeding], my mother would have beat me senseless.

Kimberly linked her Aboriginal status to breast milk and breastfeeding as a traditional food source and practice:

> It was always breastfeeding in our family; we never gave the bottle ... My son was breastfed till he was nine months; the oldest, my daughter, was breastfed till she was two, and he was breastfed till he was nine months. We were brought up traditionally. Traditionally, they should be given breastfed milk; it is there, and that is what it is there for. It's natural.

Finally, ideas about breastfeeding also included beliefs about mother–child attachment. Cathy lamented what she perceived as poor bonding with her first child because of not breastfeeding, saying, "I didn't have any sort of connection with my daughter. And seven years later to this day I don't have that. I bond with her, but it's not the way it should be." Beverly suggested that mothers who formula-feed are in some way denying their babies appropriate attachment. She described how formula-fed babies

> don't have the same attachment, I find. Mothers are more likely to lay their babies down and give them their bottle so that they are independently feeding, which they may feel is beneficial for them to be able to go and do stuff, but you are losing all of that attachment and that skin to skin and they don't get to listen to your heart beat, hear your breathing,

> and hear your voice, and I think that is really important for their development.

Her statement reveals that breastfeeding is sometimes thought to aid in healthy child development purely because of the feeding act, rather than the perceived health benefits of the milk. Erica also commented on how mothering is enacted through feeding: "You know it is nice, and the quiet and the feeding, and they are right there, and it is almost, it just makes you feel good because you are the one actually giving them the food, I think there is some kind of connection. It is not just feeding; it is part of being a mom."

Anne and Rosemary indicated that they had heard breastfeeding was better for developing attachment between mothers and babies but disputed the idea that it was necessary for attachment to take place. They divorced feeding methods from questions of bonding and good mothering while upholding ideas about the importance of mother–child attachment. Anne described it this way:

> I don't think there is a right way [to feed your baby]. People think there is a right way, and there is only one way to do it. Like, they say if you breastfeed your child it gets more attached to you, you have that bond. I didn't breastfeed and me and my son have a great bond. I don't just prop him in the car seat and prop up the bottle. He was always with me when he needed to have a bottle … It is all about the parent as well. [If] the parent is too busy and they feel they have to prop the bottle, then the parent is losing out and the child is losing out on that connection, like when you are feeding and you are looking in their eyes and they are looking into your eyes. That is the bond that everyone is talking about.

Rosemary talked about the importance of the feeding relationship for attachment regardless of method: "Even when you bottle-feed them, they stare at you. They get to know you a lot more. It is a real close relationship to feed your child. So that bond is right there. It is a really close thing." She also asserted that mothers experience bonding through the process of feeding, whereas fathers bond with their babies in other ways. She contended that when her partner helped in feeding he was merely relieving her from work rather than developing father–child attachment, and that the work of infant feeding is primarily the domain of mothers for important developmental reasons.

> It wouldn't be so he gets to experience that; it would be so I get to get a break. So I wouldn't have to get up all the time in the middle of the night. It is not just to give him the experience. There are other ways that he can get involved if you are breastfeeding. For him to sit there, when I was feeding, he would sit beside me and talk to me and we would both talk to her. She would still be on my breast but she could still look both ways so it is not that you both don't get to bond. It is just that a mother and her child bond is a lot different than the father, I find.

Mothers' infant feeding beliefs and intentions were clearly influenced by messages that breastfeeding is best for infant health and that formula feeding is sub-optimal (and not just nutritionally). Their stories demonstrated that official infant feeding recommendations had been well transferred to the intended target. Even so, actual infant feeding practices were far more tied to circumstances, and specifically the social condition of poverty in which they lived. For these mothers, worry over food shortages within the home was a driving factor for breastfeeding initiation. At the same time, their low rate of exclusive breastfeeding and high rate of formula use despite the burden of its cost calls into question the extent to which breastfeeding was in fact a reliable food system. For many of the mothers, breastfeeding was challenging and hard to navigate. For some, it was impossible due to the stress under which they lived.

Breastfeeding Policy and Food Security Policy

The mothers in this study articulated ideas about breastfeeding as a food system, and some were explicit about the potential of breastfeeding to ensure infant food security. The policy and program workers I interviewed echoed this message. Further, the idea of breastfeeding as the pathway to infant food security is contained within international agreements, national and provincial government documents, and policy recommendations created by civil society organizations. While little public policy concerns both infant feeding and food security, such as there is does identify overlapping policy realms and provides some insight into how infant food insecurity due to financial constraints – vulnerability over food access, sub-optimal food quality, and hunger or risk of hunger – has been framed as a policy issue.[1]

Canada's involvement in food security policy on the international stage began with the *Universal Declaration of Human Rights* in 1948, when the United Nations first recognized food as a fundamental human right. Article 25 states:

> Everyone has the right to a standard of living adequate for the health and well-being of himself and of his family, including food, clothing, housing and medical care and necessary social services, and the right to security in the event of unemployment, sickness, disability, widowhood, old age or other lack of livelihood in circumstances beyond his control.[2]

Since then, Canada has acknowledged the right to food in subsequent international agreements. Article 11 of the *International Covenant on Economic, Social and Cultural Rights* stresses that it is a human right to be free from hunger and that state parties will commit themselves to addressing hunger through improving food systems and food access.[3] The covenant makes no specific mention of infant feeding, but Article 10 articulates special protection for mothers in reference to social security benefits. A note on infant feeding did appear in the 1999 *General Comment No. 12: The Right to Adequate Food,* in which the United Nations Committee on Economic, Social and Cultural Rights describes breastfeeding as an appropriate consumption and feeding pattern "which may require attention." It specifies that the United Nations should assist in the drafting and reviewing of legislative frameworks (through its agencies the Food and Agricultural Organization and the United Nations Children's Fund, or UNICEF) "with regard to the right to adequate food for infants and young children through maternal and child protection including legislation to enable breastfeeding, and with regard to the regulation of marketing of breast milk substitutes."[4]

With respect to the role of parents in child food security, Objective 1.4 of the *World Food Summit Plan of Action* acknowledges the special contribution that women make to ensuring childhood nutrition, with particular mention of breastfeeding.[5] Article 24 of the *Convention on the Rights of the Child* articulates food as a human rights issue, linking children's health with food security, noting that parents need access to knowledge and support in child nutrition, and outlining the advantages of breastfeeding.[6]

Concerning international breastfeeding policy specifically, the World Health Organization (WHO) and UNICEF (though they do not use the term *food security*) have been pivotal in policy work to ensure optimal infant nutrition and feeding practices, through the *International Code of Marketing of Breast-Milk Substitutes;* the *Innocenti Declaration: On the Protection, Promotion and Support of Breastfeeding; Innocenti Declaration 2005: On Infant and Young Child Feeding;* and the Baby-Friendly Hospital Initiative.[7] Such codes, recommendations, and declarations explicitly state that optimal infant feeding and nutrition cannot be divorced from the health and nutrition of mothers and that wider social and economic barriers to breastfeeding must be addressed.

Nationally, the *Canadian Charter of Rights and Freedoms* includes the right to life and equality but does not mention the right to food.[8] *Canada's Action Plan for Food Security* outlines issues of food insecurity domestically and abroad, and assigns priority to improving food systems and food access.[9] The document identifies infant feeding as a food security concern and breastfeeding as a key strategy for infant food security, especially in developing countries:

> Breastfeeding is also highlighted as critical to infant health and nutrition worldwide. In Canada, commitment to this is furthered through actions to support working mothers, hospital programs, mother and child health care and other initiatives in support of the International Code of Marketing of Breast-milk Substitutes. Beyond the promotion and protection of breastfeeding and other food security conditions, caring practices, and health and education measures are important for the nutrition security of mothers and children, particularly, but not only, in developing countries.[10]

Although food security policy identifies breastfeeding as the route to infant food security, the actual policies surrounding breastfeeding lie within health policy domains. The WHO and UNICEF figure prominently, and their work has been translated into Canadian national policy. Such policy is guided by Health Canada, whose recommendations for healthy full-term infants call for exclusive breastfeeding for the first six months of life.[11] Health Canada also led the establishment of the Breastfeeding Committee for Canada (BCC), which oversees the assessment and application of the Baby-Friendly Initiative (BFI) nationally.

Launched in 1998, the BFI has been implemented by the provinces and territories.[12] Its aim is to facilitate initiatives and resolutions to support breastfeeding through "health promotion, education and collaboration, rather than through legislation or regulations."[13] The BFI in Canada was adapted from the Baby-Friendly Hospital Initiative launched in 1991 by the WHO and UNICEF. The term *baby-friendly* refers to protecting, promoting, and supporting breastfeeding, partly through adherence to the 1981 WHO *International Code of Marketing of Breast-Milk Substitutes*, making some aspects of breastfeeding policy a reaction to the marketing practices of formula companies.

In Canada, certain national civil bodies serve as networking, educational, and policy-monitoring organizations concerned with both food security and infant feeding. Food Secure Canada and Infact Canada have explicitly articulated a link between food security and breastfeeding. In an attempt to protect breastfeeding, Infact Canada has publicly linked formula feeding to infant food insecurity due to its high cost, stating a paradox: "Those who choose to formula feed are often those who can least afford its consequences."[14] The website of Food Secure Canada, a national registered non-profit organization, has used breastfeeding as an illustrative example of a sustainable food system:

> The consumer is in control; the food is designed to meet the specific needs of the consumer, and changes in quality and quantity as those needs change over time ... There is no excess packaging ... There is a direct, not to say intimate, relationship between producer and consumer ... Once [the system] is established, both producer and consumer derive benefits and indeed pleasure from it; and finally, the producer needs to be healthy and well-nourished or the system does not work.[15]

This description positions breastfeeding as a simplified food system that is environmentally sustainable, reliable, self-regulating, and socially sustainable through a direct relationship between producer and consumer. Food Secure Canada also led the collaborative development of *Resetting the Table: A People's Food Policy for Canada,* which states that "inadequate perinatal nutrition and breastfeeding, premature weaning, and reliance on processed commercial infant and baby food" across all income levels is linked to chronic health problems and that food insecurity is linked to poorer infant feeding practices.[16]

Provincial and territorial governments play an important role in addressing food insecurity in their jurisdictions. Most policy that has the potential to improve conditions of infant food insecurity directly is legislated and/or implemented at the provincial level through the delivery of health care and social services. The diversity and number of provincial policy measures vary by province. Policies and programs related to income security – provincial and territorial cash transfers and services, minimum wage legislation, income assistance, maternity leave – have the potential to prevent household food insecurity, and such initiatives were the most noted by the mothers in discussions about poverty and food insecurity. In Nova Scotia, as in other Canadian provinces, food security is explicitly discussed in the provincial nutrition strategy, but matters specific to feeding a baby in food insecure conditions are largely absent from such documents.[17]

While it could be argued that policy to address *infant* food insecurity does exist marginally within provincial welfare policy (such as special prenatal and postnatal diet allowances for mothers, and some provision for specialty formula purchases *if* medically indicated), most of it falls into health policy domains and is focused on breastfeeding, rather than infant feeding. Such policy includes the regulation of infant formula, not broader questions of infants' access to food in food insecure households.

Ruth Lawrence, a medical doctor who has written extensively on breastfeeding, states that breastfeeding can provide the "best nutrition" and "greatest food security" for children living in poverty.[18] But low-income mothers cannot solve poverty in their daily lives by breastfeeding. Their agency, resilience, and successes in their work to produce food must be acknowledged, but individualized food practices such as breastfeeding cannot solve the systemic problem of poverty that is itself a barrier to breastfeeding success.

3

When Breastfeeding Fails

AN INSECURE FOOD SYSTEM

> I don't know if what I was producing was really enough, nutrient wise, if it was – How would you put it? – healthy enough for him, giving him what he needed. Plus, in order to be able to produce milk, the mother needs to be food secure and you don't have that all the time, and the situation could change for you on the drop of a dime.
>
> – MARY

Food work has the power to evoke feelings of both pleasure and anxiety for mothers, and this ambivalence is no less apparent with respect to food production via the breast. Although in interviews mothers expressed a belief that breast was best, a distance existed between belief, intentions, and actual feeding practice. When mothers were successfully breastfeeding, their worry over food access, so prevalent in their stories about household food insecurity, was suspended for their babies. The food security provided by breastfeeding was highly situational, however, and subject to breakdown. Most of the infants were fed formula at some point throughout their first year, and close to a third were either exclusively or mostly formula fed. Thus breastfeeding was equally experienced as an insecure food system.

These stories encapsulate opposite responses to the question of whether breastfeeding is the answer to infant food security. For some mothers, *yes,* breastfeeding was a sustainable food system and thus a successful food security strategy. For others, *no,* they did not use breastfeeding as a food security strategy – yet they gave precisely the same reasons for their choice as the women who did so. In both cases, feeding decisions were shaped by household and maternal food insecurity, along with the desire to optimize a healthy and sustainable food source for the infants. How can this complex link between breastfeeding and household food insecurity be explained?

Early Cessation of Breastfeeding

Chapter 2 detailed the ways in which household food insecurity contributed to high breastfeeding initiation rates, but initiation is only one piece of the puzzle. Reasons for not breastfeeding and for stopping breastfeeding early tell a different story. Both are regularly monitored by the Canadian Community Health Survey (CCHS). Health Canada reports that the top three reasons for not beginning to breastfeed are the idea that bottle feeding is easier (28.8 percent), a mother's medical condition (19.2 percent), and the thought of breastfeeding as unappealing (16.7 percent). The top three responses for early breastfeeding cessation are insufficient breast milk (23.4 percent), the belief that the baby is ready for solid food (15.9 percent), and self-weaning by the infant (12.2 percent).[1] What these statistics do not tell us is what makes something easy or unappealing, what leads to not having enough milk, or what makes mother believe that their infants are ready for a different type of food. How might food insecurity help us to conceptualize and interpret these reasons?

Mothers' stories revealed both commonalities and dissimilarities over deciding not to breastfeed. Only six of the sixty-one children were never put to the breast, yet seventeen of the twenty mothers stopped breastfeeding at least one of their babies prior to six months. In the rare cases of not initiating breastfeeding, mothers explained that the practice was "not for me" (perhaps similar to finding breastfeeding unappealing), or that it had previously been experienced as "too stressful," or that it was thought to be "too much work" in light of current living circumstances. Single mothers with other young children particularly noted the latter point.[2] For example, Emily, Elaine and Jessica had no intentions of breastfeeding. In talking about her most recent child, Emily stated,

> I knew I wasn't going to breastfeed her. She was on formula and she just come off it yesterday, and is on homogenized milk. I breastfed with my first one, and it just wasn't ... I found it hard, for maybe a month and I

> was only seventeen. [I tried to breastfeed my first baby] because he was only five pounds and was small, and they said it was the best for him, so I said, "Well, I'll try it," and I tried it, and I found it was stressful on me.

Even though Elaine attempted once to breastfeed her second child, she ascribed her decision to bottle feed to discomfort:

> I don't know, breastfeeding? I don't think it's for me, and I know everybody is like, "Oh well, you should breastfeed, it is better for your babies." Well, that's fine, but I have to be comfortable doing it and I'm not. With my four-month-old I tried to breastfeed and she wouldn't latch on properly and I wasn't comfortable with it.

Similar to those who described breastfeeding as a family or cultural practice, some women identified formula feeding as family-based feeding practice, shaping their choice to do the same despite accepting the belief that breastfeeding was the best option. Rosemary, when discussing the experience of feeding her first child, explained, "My mother and my sister, they all bottle fed. They didn't try to breastfeed at all. And only one of my friends breastfed, so I was more comfortable bottle feeding. I wasn't comfortable about breastfeeding because I didn't know anything about it. So I just didn't want to breastfeed at all."

Although none of the women gave a medical condition as a factor in failing to initiate breastfeeding, Mary noted this as her reason for stopping breastfeeding early: "I nursed all them, except for [one child]. I didn't nurse him very long because of the experience I had after I delivered him. It was too draining on me." Cathy also stopped breastfeeding early because she thought the medication she had been prescribed was negatively affecting her baby via breast milk:

> I had a C-section with her, and I went through a lot; I was still in pain two and a half months after I had her. They wouldn't give me nothing for it but penicillin. Then the penicillin broke out on her bum and her face because I was feeding her. They wouldn't give me anything for pain, and I was in so much pain. I was losing a whack of weight. [The baby] was taking it in, too; it was going to her. I felt bad that she had to go through that because of me so I switched her. I also switched because I couldn't stand the pain any more.

The baby's medical condition was also noted as a reason for stopping breastfeeding. Rosemary did not want to breastfeed because her baby was tongue-tied and she did not want to snip the tongue, a procedure that may have improved the baby's latch.

Mothers did not mention their children being ready for solid food as a reason for ceasing to breastfeed, although it was noted once as a reason for discontinuing formula use early. Only two mothers, Emma and Margaret, talked about their babies self-weaning prior to their own desire to stop breastfeeding. Emma said that her second baby "had an aversion to the breast, didn't want it." Here, the food supply was insecure because it was subject to infant participation. Margaret's experience was similar:

> With my first son, my milk supply went. Now, with this baby, he is taking himself off of me. That's not my fault. I do everything I can to keep them going. If [the baby] would breastfeed I would be happier. But it doesn't work that way. So we had to start giving some formula. He does not want to breastfeed, which I am devastated about. But he apparently is not.

Mothers referred to stress over feeding and caring work as other reasons for stopping breastfeeding. Anne, for example, felt she didn't have the support she needed: "I could have stuck it out but I was busy at that time, way too much and it was just, it hurt like, it hurt a lot, and I didn't have the support where I could have, like nobody really taught me how to do it, so then I just stopped." Heather also cited caring work as the reason she stopped breastfeeding her third child:

> The first one, I didn't try because of the state of life that I was in. The second guy, I tried for about a month to breastfeed him. But he was in the hospital for a long time so I kind of gave up. He had a heart murmur. The third guy I did for about two months and then having three kids kind of overwhelmed me so I went to formula. When you are breastfeeding, you have to sit down and hold him. Then I got two other ones running around and I have to be there for 45 minutes feeding him. Honestly, with a bottle I can put him down with a bottle and prop it up and run for another one. At that time it made sense. I need to do this.

Other breastfeeding problems were mentioned, particularly problems with latch or infections. "I breastfed her for the first five weeks," Rosemary explained, "but then my breast got really sore because she wasn't latching properly, so I gave up ... I knew a lot about it, but actually doing it, that was really confusing. And with bottle feeding it is just one straight way. It is measured."

Elaine, Heather, and Angela stopped breastfeeding because of psychological discomfort. Heather described her self-consciousness: "I tried it and I didn't feel comfortable. I wanted to but then to do it ... I don't know. I don't feel comfortable going out to a grocery store and pulling out my boob in front of everybody. It kind of put me back." Angela linked her discomfort with breastfeeding to her past, and noted how difficult it was to overcome a feeling of disgust:

> A lot of my issues had to do with fear, with my past history of stuff happening to me. I feel disgusting doing it, too, and I can't jump over that fear of it. I felt I'm doing something wrong by doing it, too, no matter how much I try. It is still on your mind. And I just can't whip it out like some people do, because people will criticize you for that, too. So what are you supposed to do? You are damned if you do and damned if you don't.

Such reasons for not initiating breastfeeding or discontinuing breastfeeding suggest that despite a uniform belief that breastfeeding was best, a few of the mothers were simply disposed toward bottle feeding and the use of formula. For others, breastfeeding was negatively affected by physiological difficulties and stressful life circumstances even when they had firm intentions to do so, and this led to not having enough breast milk.

As is also reflected in national statistics, insufficient milk was the top reason mothers gave for breastfeeding cessation. What factors in the mothers' life circumstances may have caused problems with milk supply? While some noted other reasons, the primary triggers of breastfeeding cessation for this group of women were rooted in household food insecurity, maternal food insecurity and structural interference in milk production.

Milk Production Anxiety

Eight of the twenty women worried about both the quantity and the quality of milk they could produce. It is likely that most Canadian mothers, when faced with the responsibility of feeding, experience some level of fear over the possibility of a hungry baby. For the mothers I interviewed, that possibility existed against a backdrop of habitual household food shortages and hunger. Anxiety provoked by the potential for or reality of a hungry baby because of problems with milk production was at the root of breastfeeding breakdown. Susan said, "The first one, I wanted to breastfeed and I nursed him for about two weeks and I wasn't producing enough milk to satisfy him." Sally explained that she stopped breastfeeding because of insufficient milk supply:

> I planned to breastfeed my son for eight months, too, but I could only breastfeed him for two months because I dried up. My milk supply dried up and it was a sudden thing. I think my body was tired because I was only twenty-one and it was my second pregnancy in a year. I would go to feed him and he would try to eat, and he would just get mad because he wasn't getting anything, so then I got him a bottle with formula and he guzzled it all down and then I tried to use the breast pump and then nothing came out.

Heather breastfed one of her babies for a month but found she could not produce enough milk: "I found that I would breastfeed him and he would still be hungry. I couldn't produce any more than what I gave him. I always had formula in the house so I would have to make him formula and top him off with that because I never had enough."

Similarly, Susan had difficulty early on and lacked confidence in her ability to establish a sufficient supply of good-quality milk. She did not "think it was possible" to cope with demand feeding, something she thought was necessary to establish supply: "Sometimes I am busy and I will forget to have a snack here or there. Sometimes it might not be the best milk for him because I didn't eat very well that day, so he is not getting full." Because of problems establishing breastfeeding, Angela resorted to pumping her breast milk and combining breast milk and formula feeding, causing her own milk supply to diminish due to lack of demand:

> I pumped, and she drank that, and whatever else she needed I would give her formula. Then of course with pumping, your milk supply goes down, and it was getting too low down and I was getting frustrated when it

> wouldn't go back up again, so I completely took her off and switched her to formula, cause it was triple the time, when you pump and feed her and buy formula, and I was, no, I might as well do one or the other. Apparently the way the pumps draw milk is different than a baby on the nipple, so your supply goes down.

Anxiety about milk production played a role in feeding intentions as well as outcomes. Margaret feared she would not be able to produce enough milk to feed her twins and therefore did not attempt to breastfeed them. She did breastfeed her next child but supplemented the supply with formula early on because she was "too tired" to produce enough milk. Jean also planned from the beginning of her pregnancy with twins to use a mixed feeding strategy because she lacked confidence in her milk supply:

> With the first two, the twins, I was planning to breastfeed and formula-feed them. I didn't know whether I would be able to produce enough. But I had them premature. He was in the hospital for the first two months. And in the stress of one passing away, I dried up. While [the surviving twin] was in the hospital he had breast milk. I was breast pumping and sending it up. And if they didn't have enough breast milk they would feed him formula.

Jean's next child was exclusively breastfed, even though she originally intended to use a mixed feeding strategy again. Her anxiety about milk production persisted, however, and she was "constantly concerned that he is getting enough to eat," calling the issue "my one and only worry." She also noted that she would have been less concerned if she had formula-fed her son, because she would have been able to "see exactly how much he is getting and actually know he was getting this amount, and this amount of nutrients in it." Rosemary and Lorraine also worried about not being able to see how much a breastfed baby was consuming without the visual evidence of a finished bottle. Jean explained it this way:

> You can't really look at yourself, and [know] how much you are eating and whether you are eating the right thing. You wonder whether it is actually coming out in the breast milk or whether your body is sucking

> up all the nutrients. It's a paranoia. I could sit there and eat everything in my house in a day and I would still be thinking about whether he is getting enough to eat.

Jean suggested that this constant worry while breastfeeding heightened her food hoarding. Erica experienced similar worry, although she resisted attempts by health care professionals to supplement her breastfeeding with formula:

> [Public health nurses] were constantly harping on me about feeding him and that I wasn't feeding him enough. They made me feel like I was starving him to death, like I was being horrible because I wasn't feeding him enough … Even though they are saying they are pro-breastfeeding I didn't find they were. But at the same time I was thinking, "He looks fine," I didn't really agree with them. It was very stressful. I was in tears, almost ready to give up until I saw the nurse, and she was like, "He is fine," and I was okay, I could relax, I could breathe. It depends on who you talk to, even within the same organization.

Milk-production anxiety was linked to ideas about keeping the system healthy through ensuring proper nutrition for the producer, which the mothers associated with real costs. Cathy remarked, "You still have to get groceries and everything while you're breastfeeding and you have to make sure you are getting that right nutrition." Sally contested the notion that breastfeeding was a free source of food: "Technically, you do have to pay because you have to eat healthy in order to give your baby the nutrition that it needs. Breastfeeding may be cheaper than formula feeding, but it still costs." Mary commented that the cost of extra food for herself when breastfeeding was always factored into any money-saving equation: "You still have to buy food for yourself to keep yourself healthy, and the prices of fruits and vegetables and the proper meat, all that stuff you need, is really high." She also commented that the actual savings incurred by breastfeeding were marginal:

> Basically, you need to pay between $13 and $14 per can of formula. If I was buying for one baby, I would need to buy four to five cans a month,

> that is $60 to $70 a month, and that there would go toward not much, maybe a little bit of extra food to put in the house for the kids. It is not much but a little bit of a savings.

While there was some discussion about the quality of breast milk due to alcohol consumption, smoking, or medication use, most references to quality focused the nutritive value of human milk. Mary and Jessica were more concerned about this aspect than about the quantity they might be able to produce. Mary decided not to breastfeed her fourth child even though she had successfully breastfed three previous babies, because she thought that this time she might not be able to produce high-quality milk. Jessica also decided from her baby's birth that she was not going to breastfeed because her own poor nutrition made her question the quality of her milk: "I figured that it probably wouldn't be such a good idea with the way I am myself. Like, they get everything that you take and I wasn't taking what I should be taking. I wasn't eating properly and stuff and it probably wouldn't have been good for her."

Margaret expressed some relief when she stopped breastfeeding, because the combination of her own eating behaviour and worry about her baby's nutritional intake was "stressing her out." She explained that she did not eat three meals a day, although she needed to while breastfeeding: "Often I wouldn't eat all day but I had been breastfeeding him all day long and what is he getting? He can't be getting nutrition."

While supportive partners, help from family resource staff, and belief in the value of breastfeeding contributed to success for some mothers, my research suggests that maternal food security also matters. Jean, Sally, and Margaret – all breastfeeding successfully at the time of the interview although they had not done so with other children – attributed their success to a change in their family's economic circumstances. All three had previously been single, on income assistance, and using food banks but now felt more economically stable with the income support of a partner and the ability to eat better food. Hannah said her husband would take the burden of food shortage to protect her from food deprivation:

> [My husband's] way of looking at is I have to eat because I have to be able to feed the baby, so he will go without it before I go without it, and we

> try to make it so that it never happens, but there's times that the canned food, that's crap, that you get from the food bank, that will sit in our cupboard forever, he'll eat it. He has to ... If the mom doesn't have enough food to eat, then she's not going to produce milk.

Similarly, Sarah managed to make her own eating a priority despite being single, on income assistance, and experiencing household food insecurity. She stressed the importance of her own nutrition for milk production:

> I still have to eat, because I find that there's a huge difference if I don't. [The milk] may always be there but it will not fill her up. She was so cranky when I was nursing her because I wouldn't eat, so I didn't have that nutrition in my milk. And I found that when I did eat, she would be like a whole different kid and then I put two and two together. Now I eat.

Mothers emphasized that a basic level of household and maternal food security was necessary to keep lactation going and that breastfeeding was therefore not cost free.

While research indicates that breastfeeding is a robust physiological mechanism, whereby mothers do not have to be well nourished to produce breast milk, other research shows that poor maternal nutrition can lead to ill health in the mother and affect the nutritional quality of breast milk.[3] Women also require additional calories to support lactation.[4] Current medical advice asserts that *what* a breastfeeding mother eats is more important than caloric intake, however, the number of calories a lactating woman needs depends on her fat stores, her level of activity, and the nutritional value of her food intake.[5] We also know that there are constraints on the food purchases of lower-income households in Canada, particularly fruits and vegetables.[6] Food cost research in Nova Scotia has calculated that the extra food needed for a lactating mother between the ages nineteen and thirty costs $41.70 per month on top of the cost of a basic nutritious diet, which was $245.60 in 2015 for a family of four.[7] While affording formula was a struggle, some mothers perceived it as more affordable than the cost of a nutritious diet; the purchase of their own *basic,* let alone extra, healthy food was rarely a priority or even possible.

The mothers in this study overwhelmingly believed that healthy eating was necessary for successful breastfeeding. They had absorbed health and nutrition messages from health policy domains, not only about breastfeeding but also about proper maternal nutrition while breastfeeding. The structural condition of household food insecurity, however, undermined their capacity to put these beliefs into practice. Their acknowledgement of and worry about their own poor eating revealed that the reasons for breastfeeding cessation (and what might be behind the answer 'not enough milk' as the top reason for stopping breastfeeding in the Canadian Community Health Survey) require deeper examination. Stress and poor maternal nutrition are potential factors in hindering breast milk production in high-income countries.

These stories urge us to consider household and maternal food insecurity as a distinct type of worry that influences both perceived and actual poor milk production not experienced by those who are food secure. Necessity-based eating affected mothers' perceptions of their bodies; they conceived of themselves as unhealthy, with little ability to produce nutritious breast milk. Therefore, food insecurity was a threat to breastfeeding as the maternal food deprivation led women to believe that the flow of nutrients from mother to baby was compromised, and indeed sometimes did compromise it.

While individual mothers commonly referred to poor milk supply, the phenomenon has been medicalized through the diagnosis of *insufficient milk syndrome.* Critics of this diagnosis suggest that poor milk supply is largely either a misperception, a problem of technique (women are breastfeeding incorrectly), or a question of management (poor advice or separation of mother and baby within institutional medical care). They assert that with the right support, most mothers can breastfeed successfully. Much breastfeeding policy is aimed at properly supporting mothers to learn how to breastfeed, and health researchers report that an actual medical condition is in fact relatively uncommon; only 5 percent of mothers experience insufficient milk from a physical limitation.[8] Insufficient milk syndrome occurs when the mother has an inadequate amount of breast milk that could lead to *failure to thrive* in infants, a diagnosis that is itself related to "problems of milk synthesis, milk removal, or the daily infant milk intake."[9] Eight of the twenty mothers in this study indicated they did not have or feared they would not have enough milk to satisfy one of their babies. In two instances, they were prescribed medication to induce milk production, but none of the women was medically diagnosed with insufficient milk syndrome or had an infant diagnosed with failure to thrive.

It is difficult to determine the extent to which these experiences of insufficient milk were illusory or real. Looking at the issue through a sociological lens suggests that the difference matters little, as American sociologist William Thomas argues: "Situations that are defined as real are real in their consequence."[10] Furthermore, the mothers' stories challenge us to think critically about the biological reality of poor milk supply and ask what else, beyond poor breastfeeding technique, might be the cause. Anthropologist Nancy Chin suggests that rather than assuming problems with lactation are merely perception, we take women at their word and explore possible biological responses to environmental, social, and emotional toxins that might affect lactation.[11] Bio-physiological pathways of lactation are affected by health conditions known to be associated with food insecurity, such as obesity and diabetes.[12] The stories here highlight the need for more bio-physiological research on the connection between the "social toxin" of household food insecurity and lactation.

Structural Barriers to Production

Structural factors such as direct interference from hospital personnel and lack of appropriate advice and support also seem to play a role in poor milk production. Even though Emma was very educated about breastfeeding, having breastfed three children for various lengths of time, she was subjected to hospital interference in her attempt to establish breastfeeding with her fourth child:

> The nurse said, "You haven't slept at all. Why don't you put her on the bottle for the night and she'll sleep for a good four hours?" I said, "I don't think that that's a good idea because my experience with breastfeeding is that you don't do that because she can get nipple confusion," and she said "No," and I said, "Well they told me two floors down not to do that," and she said, "I don't know why they always do that. They always tell

> people that." But yeah, she got nipple confusion right at the hospital. It's not the nurse's fault – I knew better. I was exhausted and I just took a chance but she developed nipple confusion.

As a result, the baby's poor latch meant Emma could never establish breastfeeding and had to resort to pumping breast milk. She could not afford the quality breast pump she would need in order to pump long term, but fortunately she was able to borrow one from a family resource centre and continued feeding her baby in this way for two months. The breast pump was an essential item in her work for food production, yet she was acutely aware that it was the only one in the area and someone else might need it soon.

Cathy experienced interference in the hospital when a nurse fed her baby formula from a bottle without her knowledge or permission:

> I think that hospitals could help a lot but they don't always. I breastfed all my kids. I had my [now] two-year-old at 7:00 pm and they ended up taking him so I could get some sleep. Well, they didn't come get me; they fed him a bottle. They didn't wake me up. I went to sleep and woke up at 6:00 am and realized they didn't bring that baby back to me and this was hours later. So I paged the nurse: "How come my baby didn't wake up yet?" And she said we just fed him a bottle so you could sleep. "What? No, you don't do that!" So after that I wouldn't let them take him out.

Cathy also mentioned that even though she was breastfeeding, formula was placed in her room. She thought this was inappropriate, because mothers who were struggling to breastfeed might be lured by the formula through fear that their babies were hungry:

> Another thing is they put formula right underneath the cart that they put your baby in ... They usually have a little case in there if you want to use it. It would be just as easy. Because I know when I first started to breastfeed my first, it was hard. It's really hard to start. A lot of parents get frustrated, so it would be very easy, especially if you were a young mother that doesn't have patience, to just go and give the baby a bottle.

Relatedly, Lorraine described her experience of trying to learn to breastfeed in hospital with little information and support:

> I think that being educated is a very important thing because there were so many things I was never told. I was confused by it and nobody really told me anything. They kept coming in saying, "Why aren't you feeding your baby?" and I was like, "Because I don't have any milk," and they said, "Well, you should still be trying to feed her." I thought there's nothing coming out, so can I just give her a bottle? They were like, "Okay." They didn't really help me. I thought that if your milk supply was a little bit lower that it was always going to be lower. I didn't realize that the more I fed her, the more milk I would make … I assumed my milk would just come in and when it does I can just breastfeed her, but until it comes in I have to give her the formula, but your milk's not going to come in unless you're trying to breastfeed.

Lorraine was fortunate that a home visitor from public health explained what she needed to do and helped her with feeding technique, so that she was eventually able to establish breastfeeding and abandon formula use.

These institutional barriers to breastfeeding contravene the spirit of provincial breastfeeding policies to facilitate the implementation of the BFI in hospitals and in the community. At the time of the interviews, Nova Scotia had no designated baby-friendly hospitals. Ten steps must be implemented prior to a hospital achieving that status, including not giving an infant food or drink other than breast milk unless medically indicated, keeping the mother and baby together twenty-four hours a day, and giving no artificial teats or pacifiers. The stories above show that within some health care institutions, these steps are not being followed.

Structural barriers outside health care institutions also impede milk production. For example, another BFI directive is that a mother must be shown how to maintain lactation if she is separated from her baby – but the issue is not simply one of education. Three mothers in the study explained how poverty-related conditions created an insurmountable barrier to lactation during separation from their infants. Heather, Sally, and Jean had babies who were hospitalized after birth. None was able to maintain breastfeeding or the feeding of breast milk, because of the high cost of travel to the hospital from rural areas of the province. "When the twins were in the city at the [children's hospital], I was on social assistance," Jean said. "They would only pay $150/month for transportation, which is only three trips a month, to go see my kids and take breast milk. That's it!" Heather said her baby was fed formula by hospital staff to supplement the supply of breast milk she brought, reinforcing her low supply.

A general lack of support for caregiving work also created structural barriers to lactation. Single mothers with multiple children had huge workloads, and some did not feel they had the support they needed to breastfeed a new baby, particularly when it might require intense demand feeding in the early weeks to establish their milk supply. Phrases such as "I didn't think I would have the time" and "I had no support from anyone" were common. Sally described purposely teaching her baby to take a bottle so she could keep up with the demands of care work:

> I was trying to get her on a bottle from when she was six weeks old because it was just very hard for me to look after a little baby that's very high demand and then two other kids. I was by myself 85 percent of the time. I was trying to switch her over but she wouldn't take a bottle; but finally she did take a bottle. It was too hard trying to keep up on everyday household things and kids while you have a baby eating from you every hour.

Considering structures of support more broadly, there was a good deal of contradiction when it came to breastfeeding. Public health discourse encouraged the practice, social discourse criticized women for behaviours such as breastfeeding in public, and even medical discourse sometimes interfered when women persisted with breastfeeding. Conversely, Rosemary felt judged for not breastfeeding in hospital: "If you don't breastfeed they kind of look down on you. They say, 'You can do it, and why aren't you?'" Angela pointed out that women are often judged no matter which type of feeding practice they employ: "I find the people that breastfeed judge you for formula feeding, and I find that people that don't breastfeed judge people that do breastfeed because they are breastfeeding wherever." Kimberly, Mary, Hannah, and Sally also talked about negative public reaction to their breastfeeding, revealing that they had been pressured to hide themselves away (typically being asked to go to the washroom) when they breastfed in restaurants or outdoor public spaces. Hannah explained:

> People give you dirty looks all the time. It drives me insane. You would think that I was doing something dirty when I am breastfeeding, instead of being a mom and taking care of a child the best possible way. I have had people ask me to go inside while I was waiting for my cab outside the grocery store. Another time at the mall two old ladies commented that it was disgusting, and I sat down and I lifted up my top and started breastfeeding right there. I didn't bother trying to cover myself or anything, and I just looked at her and said, "How about you go eat in the bathroom?" and they both got up and walked away. They were really disgusted with me.

Only one mother, Beverly, indicated that she thought people were proud of her for breastfeeding, but she was describing how she felt about breastfeeding at the family resource centre: "This is the place, other than home, that I feel most comfortable breastfeeding, because I don't feel like I am being judged, I feel like people are looking at me with pride in their eyes: 'Yes, you did it, you are doing it. Good for you.'"

Does Breastfeeding Policy Address Infant Food Security Effectively?

While there is some evidence that breastfeeding is recognized within public policy as both a food system and the pathway to infant food security, as discussed earlier it is largely assigned to the health policy domain: specifically, breastfeeding promotion and protection. Both mothers and policy and program workers highlighted in interviews that breastfeeding policy can help set the conditions for infant food security. A policy worker from the Department of Health and Wellness indicated that Nova Scotia's breastfeeding policy governs infant feeding policy in the province.[13] This policy follows protocols established by the Baby-Friendly Hospital Initiative of the World Health Organization and UNICEF, the *International Code of Marketing of Breast-Milk Substitutes* – which policy workers described as "created to remove the influence of marketing on a mother's ability to make an informed choice about feeding her baby" – and the Breastfeeding

Committee for Canada's Seven Point Plan for the Protection, Promotion and Support of Breastfeeding in Community Health Services.[14]

Nova Scotia's breastfeeding policy is also in line with its nutrition strategy, which identifies food security and the promotion and support of breastfeeding as two of four priorities.[15] The women I spoke with didn't mention either of these documents, although their stories demonstrate that they experienced some effects of the policies firsthand. Their conversation provided evidence of positive uptake of the provincial breastfeeding policy through support received within hospital and at home through public health services and family resource centres. For example, successful breastfeeders Heather, Emma, Erica, Sarah, Beverly, and Hannah discussed the important role of breastfeeding policy (as realized through practice or in written form) in relation to support for initiating and/or continuing to breastfeed. This policy was transmitted through a combination of hospital services, feeding resource publications, home visits from family resource staff and public health staff, family resource and public health programs, and family physicians. Heather, Emma, and Erica felt supported during their hospital stays and well after through a range of community-based services, as Heather articulated:

> I found that the nurses were pretty good at helping because I couldn't get him to latch good. Yah, they were great. They do give you a little bit [of information on feeding babies] when you leave the hospital, but it is just papers. With the first one [I got help] when she was about two weeks. I can't remember what came first, but the family centre contacted me and public health contacted me. And then it just went from there. I started getting a community home visitor and public health would stop in. So between the two I was getting information about breastfeeding. I found public health and the family centre very supportive of whatever I wanted to do.

Sarah and Beverly praised the breastfeeding support they received from their local family resource centres. Beverly remarked that the family resource centre didn't promote formula feeding but was

> very pro-breastfeeding. I don't think anybody would look down on somebody that didn't breastfeed, but at the same time they don't promote

it. I think a lot of women here feel very strongly about wanting to go back to the way it was, the way it should be, and I feel that we really educate our moms here about the benefits [of breastfeeding], and we offer a lot of support, whether it is verbal support or physically helping the moms when they first have their babies.

Mothers also spoke of printed information they received from public health services. Hannah found the material on breastfeeding particularly helpful:

HANNAH: I [fed my baby] by the book.

LESLEY: So, when you say "the book" – what book?

HANNAH: Those books [indicating books in the room]. Those books right there. Those are the new ones. They gave me those.

LESLEY: Who gave them to you?

HANNAH: Those ones were from the head nurse in the hospital – there. Last time it was [the public health nurse] ... I fell right in love with [the public health home visitor] and she gave us all the information with [my last child] ... Any information I wanted to find out, if I couldn't find it on my own, I would just ask [her].

Jean, however, said she had received the books but never read them:

JEAN: They give you [a book about] newborns and they tell all about newborns and what to feed them and blah, blah, blah. Then they give you [a book about babies] *Zero to 6 Months,* I think, and then *6 to 12 Months* ... They're nutrition guides. I never read them, though.

LESLEY: None of them?

JEAN: No

LESLEY: Why?

JEAN: Because I pretty much know my kids and I know what's healthy and what's not healthy, you know?

Yet despite acknowledged support, breastfeeding policy was not always effective in its goals. As some of the mothers' stories showed, hospital services created barriers to breastfeeding success, in particular by violating step six of *Ten Steps to Successful Breastfeeding* (give newborn infants no food or drink other than breast milk unless medically indicated) and the minimum global criteria for attaining baby-friendly hospital status: to keep infant formula cans and prepared bottles of formula out of view unless in use.[16] My conversations with policy enactors highlighted that the biggest challenges in promoting and supporting breastfeeding were anti-breastfeeding cultural norms and the power of big business in the marketing of formula. A family resource worker said, "I could talk for hours about the inadequacies of breastfeeding support in communities and this country," and a policy worker from the provincial Department of Health suggested that from her perspective, formula companies were the worst culprits in setting the conditions for infant food insecurity as they had endless resources to promote the use of their products. She thought that such marketing power created an uphill battle for those establishing policy and those working directly with families in supporting breastfeeding.

Yet although mothers acknowledged the importance of breastfeeding policy, and some policy workers saw it as the necessary focal point of infant food insecurity, the women's stories suggest that breastfeeding policy in isolation is not enough to support the practice in conditions of poverty and food insecurity. Such policy by and large is not framed to address the structural issues (particularly those provoked by poverty and food insecurity) that hinder breastfeeding as a secure, reliable, and resilient food production system.

The disjuncture between beliefs about proper infant feeding, intentions, and outcomes reveals that infant feeding practices are shaped by intersecting social, cultural, institutional, and corporate relations. Existing breastfeeding policy addresses aspects of these relations in some ways, but it does not address the economic relations that underpin breastfeeding outcomes. These include inadequate welfare support, low wages and poor labour market attachments, lack of maternity protection, the neo-liberal approach of minimal state economic support for social reproduction, and a lack of collective responsibility for the welfare of children (or of all citizens, for that matter). All these factors were embodied within breastfeeding experiences, and all of them created "social toxins" that compromised milk production. Food insecurity provoked common experiences whereby these social conditions found their way into mothers' feeding practices, which in turn resulted in compromised lactation/food production. Combined with direct institutional interference and perceptions of the unproductive breast, structures and policies were manifested as biological realities.

This research is congruent with other social science research that has revealed extensive evidence of personal and societal barriers to food production via the breast. As the mothers' stories here show on a personal level, perceived and actually insufficient milk supply, latching difficulties, embarrassment, medical issues of both mothers and babies, infant self-weaning, and the need to stop breastfeeding to return to work all played a role.

On a structural level, the effect of food insecurity on infant feeding has not received much research attention outside developing countries. A Quebec study in 1998–2002 found breastfeeding to four months was less common among infants in households with insufficient food than in those with adequate food supply but the difference was not statistically significant.[17] Interestingly, a study of Canadian Inuit households in which breastfeeding was an established practice, found that it was undertaken for longer in families that experienced food insecurity, although again the difference was not statistically significant.[18] Most notable is recent reporting on the breastfeeding experiences of 10,450 Canadian women. The research demonstrates that mothers caring for infants in food-insecure households attempt to follow infant feeding recommendations but are less able to sustain exclusive breastfeeding than food-secure women are, quantifying the stories told here.[19]

Infant feeding literature that analyzes health policy specifically has called attention to the need to address the non-nutritional considerations of infant feeding decisions. Martha Morrow and Simon Barraclough's 1993 analysis of infant feeding policy in Australia notes, "Social, economic, cultural and environmental factors need to be acknowledged by those making policy if breastfeeding promotional strategies are to be made more effective."[20] Deborah McCarter-Spaulding identified public health initiatives that seek to improve breastfeeding rates within the framework of health promotion but whose efforts are focused largely on education and counselling.[21] Her findings are reminiscent of policy responses to general nutritional inequalities in high-income countries that focus on individual food consumption practice linked to diet and lifestyle. This approach is framed by what Elizabeth Dowler, a sociologist who served on the UK Food Ethics Council for many years, describes as a "rather reductionist, medical model of health to secure nutritional adequacy and appropriate dietary patterns through changing personal behaviors."[22] While we know that diet, as a component of lifestyle, is shaped by material conditions, the nutritional inequalities that result are narrowly addressed by policy.[23] There is an absence of sociological understanding of practice within lifestyle policy approaches. Initiating or not initiating breastfeeding, or stopping breastfeeding early, are issues defined by and large as a problem of motherhood; individualized infant feeding practice is targeted for intervention at the expense of policy development truly aimed at *enabling* breastfeeding. Governments have largely ignored the structural determinants of food access and the policy goals necessary to address them. The same can be said for the structural determinants of successful breastfeeding.

Among the women I interviewed, breastfeeding occurred as part of an overall family food practice in which economic circumstances shaped not only how everyone ate but also, for the mother–infant dyad, the success of lactation as a food production system. Such experiences raise questions about the likelihood of sustaining breastfeeding as a food production system in contemporary society when such work is not valued or supported economically. Breastfeeding might in theory constitute an environmentally, economically, and socially sustainable food system, but in practice economic and social constraints abound. Food security is crucial for breastfeeding success. As Vanessa Maher notes, regardless of where one lives in the world, "political and economic insecurity, ill health and overwork of mothers, gender inequality and the dangerous unhygienic environment that goes with sheer poverty" adversely affect the success of breastfeeding.[24] The individual experiences of the women in this study, along with statistics on breastfeeding duration in Canada today, suggest that an infant's access to breast milk as the "best" and "only" food in the first six months of life is not secure. Exclusive breastfeeding is largely unsustainable for many women.

4

The Bottle for Baby

FORMULA FEEDING IN FOOD INSECURE FAMILIES

> You can get formula at the food bank, and at [the church], and the [family resource centre]. My last resource would be an acquaintance. I think I might have gotten it from public health maybe once. You take what you can get. It could be just the option of being able to feed the baby. This is what I got, this is what you get.
>
> – HEATHER

Despite a high breastfeeding initiation rate and a moderately high breastfeeding duration rate, the group of women I interviewed made extensive use of formula. Thirteen mothers turned to formula at one time or another because of breastfeeding breakdown, and another three relied completely on formula.

Like breastfeeding, formula use brought feelings of both security and insecurity. At times, it was experienced as a relief from the routine worry of lactating women concerning insufficient milk supply. For women with habitual fears about being able to fill their children's bellies, it is understandable that a baby's consumption of a bottle of formula would quiet that anxiety.[1] Lorraine and Jean talked about the assurance of knowing that the baby must be full, and Lorraine asserted that food in the belly was her fundamental philosophy: "The most important thing is your child is fed. Formula or breast, it doesn't really matter; the kid is fed." Jean said, "You know what you are getting with formula." Formula offered essential security in keeping infants nourished and, in the case of one family, for toddlers as well when charity-supplied formula was used to supplement their diets.

On the other side of the coin, the women spoke of two significant problems related to infant food insecurity when a mother did not breastfeed or was unable to sustain milk production: a baby's poor health in reaction to inconsistent formula feeding; and the inability to afford formula.

Formula As a Health Problem

Several mothers had trouble getting their babies to adjust to formula. For example, Jessica said her baby "had trouble digesting it, and it wasn't agreeing with her bowels." Negative reactions to one type of formula usually led to trial and error to find a more suitable brand. When Rosemary switched her baby to formula she was at first relieved, believing that it would provide a sufficient quantity of food, but then she worried about what the formula was doing to her baby, who became very constipated and "projectile vomited." Her physician decided that the baby had a milk allergy and needed soy-based formula. Rosemary asked, "If breast milk and soy doesn't work, what is the next step? It is frustrating and confusing because you don't know what is going to happen." Heather concurred: "I think I went to two or three different formulas because he was always bringing it back up, so I would have to switch him between formulas and see." Sally's baby drank four different formulas in a short period:

> He started off on [one type] at two months. He was extremely constipated and couldn't have a bowel movement because it was all just stuck in there, so I took him to the doctor and the doctor said change it to a low-iron formula. So I did that and I put him on [another type of formula] and it still bound him up and gave him acid reflux. So I switched to [another type] and I found out that it is the same as [the first formula], so then I switched to [a soy-based formula] which finally worked.

Emma also had issues with milk-based formulas. She said that her baby "would just scream hysterically. He was so unhappy, miserable, and you could just see that he was in pain." Eventually Emma switched her baby to soy-based formula.

Susan described the process of finding the right formula as a "nightmare" and full of conflicting advice:

> I have been through every kind of formula there is with the three of them … The doctor gave me a big list of all these things I should do. Not one of them has worked and all it has done is make it worse. When you change their formula so much it is hard on their stomach, too, because they just get used to one but the doctors will recommend you to do these things and you do what the doctor tells you to do, but it doesn't work so you go to a different doctor. Every doctor and nurse and pediatrician, they all have something different to tell you. A nurse told to not give him water. Water will take away from their eating. Another nurse told me that water is really good to keep them flushed, so you never know what you are supposed to do. So now I just try it. If it doesn't work, I don't try it no more.

Some women compared formula feeding unfavourably with breastfeeding. Angela said that her baby "hated the formula. She used to scream. She would throw up a lot, get really gassy." She compared this to when the baby was breastfeeding: "She was fine, she was happy, she was content. She was constantly hungry but she was happy." Sally commented that it was difficult to get help dealing with negative outcomes of formula: "If you are going to formula-feed they pretty much say, 'Here's your formula,' but with breastfeeding they have a consultant in the hospital to help you and if you are having troubles you can come back and they will sit in the room with you and help you try to feed your baby."

This sentiment was echoed by staff I spoke with at two different family resource centres after conducting interviews. One staff member said home visitors were noticing that mothers encountered difficulty mixing formula because of a lack of basic cooking skills. She indicated that skills such as distinguishing standard cooking measurements were no longer taught at school and people were becoming accustomed to eating only processed food "out of boxes." She recounted that one mother she was helping did not know what a teaspoon was, and was therefore not mixing powdered formula properly. The worker worried that not providing informational support for formula feeding was putting babies at risk. Various studies have found similar evidence of inadequate information and support for mothers who decide to bottle-feed.[2] At a different centre, I was told that staff do provide programming on formula feeding even though they "have been given grief" for doing so from community-based and public health partners outside the centre who believe that providing formula information goes against provincial breastfeeding policy and the BFI.

Formula As Unaffordable

A few mothers indicated that their intentions about feeding their babies were not based on household food insecurity concerns. One said it made no difference to why she wanted to breastfeed, and three others specified that their reasons for formula feeding were not based on cost. Everyone else discussed the cost of formula at length. The economic drain of buying formula and/or the negative outcomes of not being able to afford formula were quickly realized for food insecure families. Infant food insecurity is the outcome when the price of formula is prohibitive. When Sally's milk "dried up" unexpectedly, she had to switch to formula feeding without having budgeted the cost: "Being able to afford formula was my biggest problem when I was on assistance. It was very hard to budget the monthly income that you get when spending $70 every two weeks to feed your baby just formula, not including baby food and the cereal. The cost is not cheap."

In almost every case when babies left the hospital drinking formula, their mothers changed to a cheaper brand as soon as they got home. The type used in hospital tended to be the most expensive, and Cathy suggested that this was a ploy to ensure mothers kept buying that formula when they were at home: "[The formula company] knows that if your kid has been in the hospital and drinking it for three or four days, you won't want to switch it because it might screw the baby up. Then parents will go out and pay $50 a case. I can't afford that. You would have to have some good job for that."

Going on the advice of health professionals that all formula is "pretty much the same," mothers were quick to switch to cheaper powdered formulas, usually the in-store brand. Angela said that the cheapest formula she could find that did not cause digestive issues for her baby was $43 a case, which meant that at times she had to use another, less expensive formula regardless of her baby's negative reaction. She often ran out of even the cheapest formula and had to find ways to make it stretch: "She has had to drink the no-name because that is all I had, $25 and she had to drink it. I would water it down a little bit more, or give her a little bit more juice or water. She had to drink it, because she can't go without food."

Sally, Rosemary, Susan, Heather, and Emma also noted that buying specialty formulas because their babies needed them was a problem because these brands were the most costly.[3] Emma said, "He was very sensitive to the formula so I had to put him on a soy-based formula which was extremely expensive. Eight years ago, $35 for six cans of formula for a growing baby, very expensive." The need to change formula type also meant that the inappropriate formula had to be wasted or, as in Heather's case, used anyway because there was no alternative:

> If you open up one can and it is not working, how can I go and afford another can? Yes, I'm freaking. Yes, especially when I couldn't afford to buy the first one. Then you just wasted $30 on a can of milk you can't use. I had to make him drink it, even though he was spitting it up. I don't think you are supposed to. I spent the money for it so I'm going to use it. I didn't have any other choice. Then at the end of the can or case, then I would try a different kind.

Formula needs are supported minimally by provincial governments in Canada through food entitlements for children on welfare, but not all provinces include such entitlement in their welfare policy, Nova Scotia among them. Provincial and territorial welfare programs include some special diet allowances, but infant formula is not necessarily considered a special need unless medically indicated. Again, Nova Scotia provides an example. The Canadian approach to income security broadly, and maternal/infant programs specifically, differs from that of other, similar high-income countries in its relative lack of targeted food entitlements. Unlike in the United States and the United Kingdom, there are no state-provided food programs for infants, either federally or provincially. Women, Infants, and Children (WIC), a supplemental nutrition program in the United States that promotes and protects breastfeeding within low-income populations, also provides food supplementation via vouchers for infants and children as an entitlement.[4] The UK Healthy Start Program is a similar income-targeted voucher program that aims to improve the health of pregnant women and families; the vouchers can be used to purchase milk, fruits and vegetables, and infant formula.[5] While the Canada Child Benefit is in place to support the costs of raising children in Canada, the cash transfer is not targeted to food. It may in fact be used for other household needs such as rent and heat, particularly by families receiving income assistance when their shelter allowances do not cover the real costs of housing. As Chapter 1 showed, this was routinely the case for mothers in this study.

All the women I interviewed participated in the Canadian Prenatal Nutrition Program (CPNP), which is funded and managed by the Public Health Agency of Canada (PHAC). Like the US WIC program and the UK Healthy Start Program, CPNP is intended to support vulnerable pregnant and postnatal women.[6] In agreement with critics of the WIC program, however, PHAC steers program delivery with the view that free formula distribution negatively affects mothers' choice of feeding method and lessens breastfeeding initiation rates. Infant feeding policy embraces the uniform position on promoting and supporting breastfeeding as the sole nutrition strategy for infants.[7] Steering program delivery with policy from afar typifies neo-liberal governmental approaches to meeting social welfare needs.[8]

As a result, some mothers who chose to formula-feed indicated that they were left mostly to their own devices and, when problems arose, to seek the advice of their family physicians (which they often experienced as unhelpful). Both mothers and the CPNP workers I interviewed identified a lack of informational resources on proper formula feeding. Under the directives of provincial breastfeeding policy, the documents to which parents and professionals refer had been revised to "ensure that information on breastfeeding and infant feeding is standardized" within a newly produced series of healthy child development guides. This included *Breastfeeding Basics* and four publications in the *Loving Care* series: *Birth to 6 Months, 6 to 12 months, 1 to 3 years,* and *Parents and Families*.

At the time of this research, all these care guides could be downloaded from the government of Nova Scotia website *except* for a resource for parents called *How to Feed Your Baby with Infant Formula.*[9] A provincial health policy worker remarked that this publication had not been made available in order to adhere to provincial breastfeeding policy, and specifically, its objective of supporting the implementation of the Baby-Friendly Initiative in Canada with regard to the *International Code of Marketing of Breast-Milk Substitutes.*[10] A directive from the Breastfeeding Committee of Canada states: "Women who have made an informed decision not to breastfeed receive written materials on the feeding of human milk substitutes that is current, appropriate, and separate from breastfeeding information."[11] The worker explained, "You can't get our resource on the internet. [The Department of Health and Wellness] produced the document and Public Health Services distributes the guide; each district is responsible for determining how it gets distributed." Although notionally, the guide was distributed after mothers had chosen to formula-feed, none of those I interviewed had ever received it although 85 percent of them had used formula at some point. The guide states on its opening page that it

> has been developed for parents who have made an informed decision to feed their baby with infant formula. It tells you what you need to know to feed your baby as safely as possible (how to properly mix formula, understand the feeding cues of babies and access how much is enough, and the appropriate formula to use for developmental stages).

When I asked the worker if she thought that the timing and method of distributing this guide effectively addressed mothers' needs, she said she "could argue both sides," meaning that it was effective in upholding the breastfeeding policy but that it had the potential to be ineffective if not readily available.

It is difficult to know if having this information and the support of a public health nurse would have affected the infant feeding outcomes of the mothers in this study. What *is* known is that in the absence of the booklet, they turned to the formula industry (via the labels on the can) as their main source of information on how to use formula. A guide to formula feeding that is provided only *after* the decision to do so has already been made implies that the information it contains – how much formula costs, how much work might be involved, and the equipment necessary to have on hand – is not important for informing choice.

Informational issues aside, the non-affordability of formula has consequences that are much the same as those caused by food access problems in general. It, too, leads to compromised diets for mothers and fathers, routine use of food charity, borrowing money, and stealing. Additionally, it led to three specific household food practices: a hierarchy of feeding, pathologized foraging for formula when food charity failed, and sub-optimal feeding.

Baby Comes First: A Hierarchy of Feeding

As discussed in Chapter 1, and consistent with the literature, intra-household variation in food access – whereby parents, particularly mothers, prioritize their children's food access above their own – is a feature of living in food insecure circumstances. Less is known about how the presence of an infant in the household alters this hierarchy of food access. The current study reveals that the special needs of infancy led to a hierarchy of feeding in which the baby's food access was given priority over that of other family members. The social organization of maternal food work revolved around the baby and in many ways demonstrated a distinction based on age that Anne Murcott describes as the "social place of infancy." She refers to infancy as a social status in which the body is conceived of as socially and physically immature and "being so young, being so incapable, places babies on the limits of human society." In this state, "their vulnerability finds practical expression in the extra care with which feeding and cleaning is carried out."[12] As Lorraine said, "I have a responsibility for this person that can't do anything for herself."

In terms of the social organization of the family meal, feeding the baby involved a different routine and schedule, and was made a priority. So, too, was purchasing the baby's food. Susan, Margaret, Cathy, and Jean talked about always making formula the first purchase when grocery shopping. Susan described her routine:

> When the family allowance came in I would go and buy five cans of formula. And if he happens to drink that formula I would have that extra

> can. I would make sure I had bottle liners. I would do all his shopping first. And make sure I had everything for the month first. I would get laughed at because I would have a cart full of baby food so I would know I wouldn't run out of anything. And [with] whatever [money] was left, I would go buy my groceries for everyone else.

Cathy's practice was similar, and she explained that infant food needed to be a priority because of babies' limited diet: "When I was on assistance I would shop once a month and I just made sure I bought enough formula. I pretty much fed the [other] kids what I ate. Infant wise, you generally spend a lot more on babies in general. When they got to be toddlers you could feed them different." Jean said that the price of the baby's food affected the amount of money she had to feed others:

> The one thing that I made sure I had was formula. It was the first thing that I ever bought. I would buy enough for at least a month. And if I didn't think it was enough for a month I would still buy more. I used to buy four cases every family allowance right off the bat. It impacted the money I had for other food, but at least I knew the baby was getting fed.

Making the purchase of formula a priority altered not only the diets of mothers and fathers but also those of older children. As they were able to be more flexible about food than an infant, these children shared the burden of compromised diet, although to a much lesser degree. In families with multiple children, the hierarchy of feeding began with babies' needs, followed by younger children's, and then parents' – with seemingly no difference between mothers and fathers (except in two cases, when a breastfeeding mother was prioritized over the father).

Mothers also experienced greater fear that they would run out of formula than of other food and, as a result, their anxiety about feeding infants was heightened compared to feeding other children. Infants were perceived to be fragile, more vulnerable, and in need of special attention both developmentally and because of their inability to communicate hunger. Angela explained the added worry of running out of formula: "Especially with no budget to do anything, if she runs out, what am I going to do? With the other ones, I can improvise; with a baby, you can't. If you don't have what they need, you don't have what they need."

Mothers worried that because formula is a specialized food, it cannot be found in every store, and it is the only legitimate food source for babies other than breast milk. Others in the household could eat "anything" if it was a matter of survival. As Lorraine said, "Getting formula is more stressful for sure, because if you don't have the money [for it] then you need to get it somehow and your other kids can eat something else, maybe not the healthiest thing but at least they're not going hungry." Emma and Rosemary echoed that sentiment, Rosemary noting the complication of finding formula in rural areas: "If you are bottle feeding it is like a special thing. Obviously they can't eat what everybody else is eating. If you do live outside of town you can't always come in contact with formula because it is a special thing."

Only one mother talked about an effort to secure food that was more evenly distributed across all the children in her household. With five children living with her, Mary said, "I can't look at just infant feeding, 'cause I have all them to feed. You just try to do your best, and think about what is the easiest way you can keep the most [food] in the house for all of them." Mary's decisions involved weighing choices to provide the maximum food security for all members of the family unit.

Whether it was cheaper to feed infants than older children was contested. Some found it more expensive to feed older children because they ate more and needed a large variety of foods. For example, Margaret said,

> Sometimes we start to get low on our milk. So the other kids are older. So instead of having cereal they will have waffles and we save all the milk for the baby, and every time [my partner] gets paid we make sure that the baby has seven bottles of food because he eats one per day. But the other kids you have to portion it out. I think it's easier to feed an infant than it is to feed everyone else in my house. I believe it is cheaper to buy however much formula he will need in a month and how much baby food he will eat in a month. It is harder with the older kids because they are eating a lot more. Before I used to be able to split one pork chop between three of them and now they all eat their own pork chop.

Others who spent less money on food in general, especially those who relied heavily on food charity, thought it was more of an expense to feed infants because their food was specialized.

The study suggests that in low-income households where purchasing formula was made the priority, infants were the most food-secure members of the family, with a notable exception: infants who required food charity as a last resort were clearly the most affected by the dynamics of household food insecurity.

Pathologized Foraging for Formula

The possibility of running out of formula when there was no money to buy more left some mothers in need of alternative ways to acquire it. Just as when families ran low on food in general, several options were pursued. Attempting to obtain formula through charity, however, was often a futile endeavour or came with heightened food risk. From mothers' accounts, formula was available at food banks or churches only infrequently or not at all, revealing significant differences in availability across the province. Heather, Sarah, Susan, and Margaret talked about being able to acquire formula, jarred baby food, and baby cereal from the food bank on occasion but noted it was "never a guarantee" as it depended on donations. Margaret speculated on why formula was not available at food banks: "I used to volunteer at the food bank and I don't think formula was one of the things they have there. It is because they try to give things out in tiny proportions. They can't open a can of formula and divide it out because it is only good for a month."

Susan indicated that she had to ask for it, "cause they won't just offer things like that, but if you ask them and you are almost out of diapers and formula, baby food even, and you ask them, they will go look ... They usually have jars of baby food, but formula, not so much." Most mothers did not see the need for jarred baby food, preferring to make their own, but did end up taking it from the food bank – particularly when no vegetables were available – because it was far easier to obtain than formula.

Food insecurity provoked *pathologized foraging* for formula when the product was largely inaccessible and the mother had to rely on charity. Food insecure women foraged for formula from food banks, churches, and community organizations, a process that was fraught with challenges. They were often unsuccessful or were forced to use products they knew their babies might not tolerate. Some resorted to stealing formula when it could not be found through charity sources.

Some mothers with access to this type of food charity depended on it heavily. Mary relied on charity formula regularly to supplement what she could afford: "Probably I would have to get a couple of cans … extra to manage through the month, about a third from charity. I buy about four to six cans, depending on what else I need to buy, and two to three cans from other sources." Elaine, who also routinely relied on charity, thought that the ability to obtain formula from the food bank made feeding babies easier than feeding her other children, who required multiple food items:

> When the kids were young, even up to a year, it's a lot easier feeding babies than it is to feed yourself and older children. Babies don't eat very much; they eat formula and baby food and you can get pretty much both of those at the food bank. The food bank has already given me two bags of baby food, so when she starts it I won't have to buy it for a while. They don't always have formula, but when you call them they will ask if you need formula or diapers and food, and if you say yes then they will try and accommodate you in that way.

Elaine's regular reliance on infant-specific charity explains in part why she was unconcerned about the cost of formula and did not consider it a factor in her infant feeding intentions.

Some mothers indicated that the food banks in their area never had formula and that they did not know where they could get it if they needed it and could not pay for it. Others said that when a food bank didn't have formula on site, staff would sometimes purchase it on their behalf, placing an order at a local drugstore for the mother to pick up and ensuring she received the type she needed. Mothers also reported that one never knew which type of formula would be available at a food bank; it could be any brand, milk or soy based, or designed for any developmental stage of feeding. The stock was simply whatever had been donated. The women indicated that any given food bank typically carried only one brand, and rarely the one the baby was drinking. A food bank worker confirmed the random nature of formula availability, adding that donations tended to be of brands that didn't sell well, as these are first discounted and then donated if they are reaching their expiry dates.

Such piecemeal charity resulted in mothers choosing to explore other options or taking whatever was available out of desperation, switching their baby's type of formula against their better judgment. Two mothers indicated that public health staff had told them changing brands had only a minimal effect on a baby's digestive system if the general type of formula stayed the same, but this reassurance was of limited relevance when mothers were forced to use whatever product was available. Mary remarked, "I get formula from a lot of different places. I have to switch types. Like, if I needed to get it from my doctor, they don't have the store brand. I do that once a month so then it would have to change."

Emma and Heather indicated that the formula and baby food available from charity sources had sometimes passed its expiration date. "Six times out of ten they will have [formula], and baby food," Heather said. "Most times a bit of the jar baby food or the boxes of cereal. But I found that any time I got any of it, it was expired and I couldn't use it. I would go once a month and every time it was expired."

Mary also found making baby food from food bank offerings a challenge:

> The babies are old enough now that what I cook for the older kids I feed the babies, if there is a vegetable that is good for when they are starting to eat. But there is nothing from that food bank food that you could feed a baby, except maybe stewed-down apples. You might be able to blend up the can of peas. That is why when I went today; I was not leaving there without apples. Those kids like apples, and I had to fight for them.

Mary and Hannah explained the occasional "strings attached" to getting help in feeding their babies. Both talked about a local street ministry that provided pregnancy and early-parenting support but "invited" them to pray before receiving help, and in Mary's case, to endure being prayed for:

> They have made me pray – not really made, but they ask you to pray and you know they are going to get offended if you don't, and I have had to do that to get a food voucher for formula before, and they always want

> to pray for you. These people don't even know me as a person. I'm a broke-ass woman that is basically coming in and begging you for formula for my kids. What do they know? How can they pray for me if they don't know? They say, "Can we pray for you?" Well, God hasn't been there for this amount of time and I'm thirty-three.

Alternatively, mothers sometimes sought help from the family resource centre. Angela said, "I could come here to the family resource centre and get formula if they had her brand." Hannah added, "The [staff person at the family resource centre] helped me a lot with food and infant feeding," and Mary declared, "I can always count on support from them." Sally indicated that her family resource centre would give away formula and baby food if they had it, and offered nutrition-related programming for feeding children. Susan and Rosemary said that their family resource centre had a cupboard for families to trade items, and that it always contained unexpired formula. Rosemary explained the system:

> This facility has a thing called the Trading Post. If you have an extra bag of wipes, you can trade. So it's free. For this facility, they check expiry dates. It can't be touched or broken at all. I don't know if the food bank even has it. When you are on formula you just can't give your child any formula. But here at the [family resource centre], I don't know who supplies them with it but they always have formula here. Always. I have never known a time when they haven't had it.

Mothers used various other practices to get the formula they needed.[13] For example, if they received charity formula of the wrong type, some would return it to a store in exchange for in-store credit (even without a receipt) to purchase the formula type they needed. Or charity formula was used as an exchange commodity. Mary exchanged high-priced formula she received for free from a family resource centre with lower-cost formula in order to increase the volume of food. "[The centre worker] said, 'Call and take it back and get the store brand,' and I got three times that amount of formula. They gave me a gift card at Walmart. I got twelve store-brand cans and there was still money on the card."

Mary also talked about people giving away formula or selling it cheaply on Kijiji, a Canadian online classified advertising service. When asked about this, however, some mothers commented that they were uncomfortable getting food via the Internet. Erica said, "I don't think I would be buying anything there. Like, you don't know where it has been or if it has been tampered with. I would be worried about it," and Mary asked, "Do you really know who these people are?"

These stories highlight how a food charity model of addressing household food insecurity is uniquely problematic for mothers and infants. Acquiring needed formula carried the same challenges as access to any food from charity sources, but because it was relatively expensive, formula was more difficult to obtain and subject to the vagaries of business and individual donation efforts. At the same time, it was the only food item that the majority of infants in these food insecure families ate. Heather described her feelings of desperation around feeding her babies and what food insecurity led her to do:

> We sell stuff. Steal stuff. Steal it to sell it, steal formula from the store. Whatever we had to do to feed them, we did it. I feel guilty for sitting here saying it but hey, I did it. I was sometimes to the point that you feel you have to go walk the streets to get money to feed your baby. But I couldn't put myself in that position. So we would borrow from the man walking down the street. My partner would sell something to the pawn shop to get the money to get formula. That happened quite a bit. You don't realize until you get there, "What do I do, what do I do?" You start freaking. You got no money and people won't give you any money. There is nothing at the food bank. So if I go to the store and put this can of milk in my stroller under a blanket and you can't see it and go out the door, hey, I can feed my kid now. If I am going to do that to feed him then I am going to do it.

Troubled Infant Feeding

From the stories above, we can see the limited options for families experiencing formula shortages. Even though infants tended to be a priority in household feeding, in extreme situations of food insecurity formula-fed infants – particularly those who were not yet eating solid food – were in fact the most vulnerable family members. One outcome was sub-optimal feeding practices, as liquids other than formula were introduced occasionally through the first year and sometimes before six months: water, juice, milk made from powdered milk, homogenized cow's milk, and canned evaporated milk.

These feeding decisions were based on economics, not a lack of knowledge. "There was a time with my little guy," Heather said, "when he was four months old, that I had to give him our powdered milk because I didn't have any formula. I got the powdered milk at the food bank. I switched at nine months to whole milk because it was cheaper." Cathy had a similar comment: "I know a few people that switched their kids to cow's milk because it was cheaper at a very young age. They probably didn't tell many people but I did know. I never did, though. If I know a few people, there is probably a lot more people out there that do it."

Mary at times had to feed her babies evaporated canned milk, cow's milk, or powdered milk, and she occasionally diluted formula to make it stretch when her babies were older: "I have used evaporated canned milk and had to water down formula to make it stretch sometimes. If I have whole milk in the house and I don't have [enough] formula or powdered milk I'll mix it half and half for the babies, but not when they were really little." Heather indicated the same: "I would have given them whole milk all month if that is all I had, or sometimes I would have to give them a bottle of water because I didn't have whatever. Or I would have to give a bottle of juice at two months; I would have to. I actually mixed canned milk with water a couple times."

Infant food shortage led to altered diets, whereby babies were fed whatever was available from the food bank. For example, powdered milk (usually repackaged in subdivided units) was a common food bank offering. While this might not have been intended as infant food, mothers faced with emergencies made use of it as such on occasion. The same occurred with canned evaporated milk. Heather said, "At the food bank they would give two cans of canned milk and powdered milk which, if I didn't have anything else to feed the baby, that would last me two weeks." When I accompanied Mary to the food bank, I noticed a "baby shelf" in the intake room where recipients were interviewed prior to receiving food. On the shelf were jarred baby food, diapers and other baby supplies, and a can of evaporated milk, all for mothers to take freely as needed. I asked Mary if canned milk was usually on the baby shelf, and she replied,

> It was surprising to see it there, because they usually keep it out back and that is one of the choices you pick between, canned milk or powdered milk. I would usually choose the canned milk to keep for the babies; the powdered milk they give you is just a little baggy that I could use for a day to make up bottles for the babies if I stretched it.

Regardless of whether these milk products were displayed for babies or kept in the back with the rest of the food products, some mothers used them as a last resort to feed their babies.

Free infant formula was also used well after the recommended duration as a food security strategy. Mary sought as much infant formula through charity as possible as an essential household food item because cow's milk was more difficult to get for free. Milk could be obtained only at the food bank and was needed for older children, whereas formula was sometimes available from her doctor and from churches. Mary's ability to obtain free formula highlights the inconsistency of infant food charity as well as her own resourcefulness, as she had secured sources she could count on to a certain extent, while most other women said it was either unavailable or only occasionally available in their area. Mary felt secure knowing she had formula in her cupboard, as it had a longer shelf life then cow's milk and provided a larger quantity of food when reconstituted. She breastfed most of her children for several months but then used formula as a food source well into their second and third years:

> After I was done nursing them I did use formula, and when it comes to formula, I usually keep the babies on it for a long time. I have just now taken them off formula and one is three and the other is two, because to me they still needed those nutrients and I can't keep milk in the house for them to be drinking all the time.

She also believed that formula was something of a "super food," as it added nutrition that her children's regular diet might be lacking:

> And a lot of people look at me like I'm crazy for that. I'm told that I was stupid for doing it, but look at the back of the formula package and look at the back of powdered milk. Do you think powdered milk has all this? And it is something that you can get free in more places. The kids can eat it on cereal if they needed to. Of course, then there is no milk for the other kids to have cereal so they would have to go to the breakfast program at the school.

Mary thought that her children's diet was poor because she relied heavily on food bank items, and she believed that formula provided added nutrition, based on the label claims:

> If I thought they had everything that they needed, then I wouldn't worry so much about the formula. I wouldn't bother with it, but it is one way for my youngest kids to get more food and that makes me feel a little bit better; it is something I can give them. If I feed them a can of soup from the food bank, it really isn't the healthiest thing. Look at chicken noodle soup: there are noodles in there and about five little bits of chicken, and it's full of salt. The nutrients they need really aren't there, but if that is all you have to feed them than that is what you do, and all the other nutrients that they need are in that bottle of formula.

Even though Mary was a long-term breastfeeder, she saw both breastfeeding and free formula as part of a food security strategy. Nonetheless, like breastfeeding her access to formula was time limited and vulnerable, as the food bank and the street ministry (where she was required to pray) eventually refused to give it to her:

> I used to be able to get the formula from the food bank; now they won't give it to me for the kids. They were giving me a can for one child, which was regular infant formula, and then they would give me a can for the other one, which was like for six month and up or twelve month, and then it was like, "No, we can't provide the formula any more for the kids

> because really they should be on regular milk." But they can't give me enough milk.

No other mother talked about this use of formula, although Cathy had heard of the practice of prolonged formula usage as a toddler food:

> I know a girl who kept her child on formula for quite a while because when she got her cheque you couldn't really get enough milk to do the whole month because it would go bad. But formula doesn't go bad, so she found it a lot easier to keep her on formula; in that way she wouldn't have to worry that in the middle of the month that she wouldn't have milk.

Community-Based Responses to Formula Needs

Against a backdrop of a lack of upstream income-based policy approaches to household food insecurity, interpretations of provincial breastfeeding policy that restrict information about formula feeding, and the difficulty of finding infant formula from charity sources, the mothers' stories of pathologized foraging for formula reveal serious problems of unequal food access, potential food risk, and food injustice for both mother and baby. My interviews with policy and program workers also revealed the policy tensions between breastfeeding policy (which includes the regulation of infant formula) and food-based measures to address food insecurity that incorporate the long-standing tension between supporting breastfeeding and making formula readily available.

As mentioned, CPNP programs have neither a mandate nor the resources to respond to the infant formula needs of food insecure families. Because their mandate is to support vulnerable women with children in early infancy, however, including with respect to infant feeding, CPNP workers are well aware of the needs of families struggling with such issues and may be their primary source of support. A core value of CPNP programs is that they are community based and therefore embrace the community development principle of responding to local needs. At the same time, although families within communities experience the need for formula due to poverty, providing this food is strongly advised against and is not addressed within the current funding arrangements or infant feeding policy directives of the Public Health Agency of Canada.

PHAC itself recognizes the dilemma faced by organizations in this regard and has responded with a practical guide titled *Protecting, Promoting, and Supporting Breastfeeding: A Practical Workbook for Community Based Programs*. Here is the response to infant food insecurity it suggests:

> Women who come to community based programs are often faced with financial or food insecurity that affect their ability to buy formula. Rather than giving formula directly, a better use of resources could include providing food, food coupons, recipes and ingredients, good food boxes and encouraging collective buying and community gardens. These approaches put *"Mothers and Babies First,"* help decrease the stress of food shortages, and free up the family's own money to buy formula *if needed*. Still, in spite of these strategies, staff sometimes see women who are desperately short of resources, and they fear for the adequacy or appropriateness of the baby's diet. In these situations, it is best to work with partners whose work is less directly tied to the protection, promotion and support of breastfeeding and develop an emergency response approach for babies at risk. Referral to a family physician, paediatrician, and/or dietitian may be appropriate. Linking the mother with the local health unit and area food banks may also be helpful.[14]

When it comes to infant food insecurity, the last sentence is striking; it is evident that, while supporting food supplementation for families to a certain extent, the federal government endorses a culture of food charity for infants. It views formula needs as a practical dilemma for community-based workers, not a responsibility of government to support an infant's entitlement to food.

How do CPNP projects and food banks navigate this "practical dilemma" of infant food insecurity? A social worker from a family resource centre confirmed the extent of the issue: "Off the top of my head, I cannot think of one person that we have in our program who is food secure. Not one. Not one. And we work with two or three hundred families in a year at least, probably more than that. I can't think of one." Are food banks an appropriate solution, and are they able to meet the need? And how might these organization's responses affect infants and the mothers who are ultimately held responsible for the social reproduction labour of feeding their babies in food insecure conditions in Canada?

Family resource centres and food banks bear the brunt of supporting families faced with infant food insecurity. The stories above demonstrate what mothers encountered when they needed to turn to them. They were subjected to informal and site-specific policy that shifted over time in response to various external influences. During my fieldwork for this study, five staff members from four different centres discussed with me their role in providing support for formula feeding, all describing it as a delicate balance of contradictions between breastfeeding policy, their own values, and the needs of program participants. They struggled with the issue of how to support mothers and infants in need of formula, and with their own feminist values and the policy framework within which they worked to protect breastfeeding.

One worker told me about experiencing a backlash from community partners (some of them other family resource centres) when she held a session with parents on the proper use of formula. Another discussed what she phrased as "the elephant in the room" when community partners discussed infant feeding concerns. She explained that while everyone might agree women using formula needed support, those who gave it were forced to "go underground," providing formula "on the down low." The centre where she worked had taken a bold stance by creating a sharing cupboard for baby items, and she ensured it always contained formula – particularly as her local food bank never carried formula because of pressure from the local hospital to be "baby friendly." The food bank instead referred clients to the family resource centre or to the occasional physician or public health nurse.

One interviewed worker articulated a conflict between her role as a lactation consultant and her commitment to supporting women in feeding their babies within impoverished environments:

> I prefer that people breastfeed, and I think that is the ultimate thing for an infant. I think about breastfeeding in terms of that it can provide infant food security, but the definition for me of infant food security would be

> that an infant would have access to food that they need to grow and develop normally without it being compromised in any way. Breastfeeding is not the choice that people always make, and a lot of people that we work with don't make that choice. Or they make that choice initially and then things change, and when someone calls me and says "I don't have any formula," I have to do something about it.

Her co-worker explained that they "get those calls, often" and that they "are left scrambling trying to find formula for the babies." She said that workers often bought formula, sometimes out of their own personal funds, after exhausting other possibilities such as getting it from doctors, qualifying the practice: "I know that we shouldn't and we aren't supposed to, but we do because what else can you do?" After, I asked her what she meant when she said she and colleagues weren't supposed to provide formula. She responded, "Well, I think that – I don't know who said that we are not supposed to – but I am not going to say to [our funders] like, 'Hey, listen, we're buying formula for babies.' I just don't talk about it. I don't ask for permission. We just do it if we can't access anything else."

The co-workers in this interview were personally uncomfortable about providing formula. One family resource worker who was also a lactation consultant said that getting formula from physicians' offices was not ideal because it was usually not the type of formula needed by the mother. She saw a mother's need to switch formula because of such offerings as contributing to infant food insecurity because it disrupted the infant's digestive system. Every time she found formula for a mother, she stipulated, "This isn't something that we do" to indicate she was contravening official policy within her organization. I asked her to explain her personal discomfort further:

> LESLEY: When it comes to purchasing formula, what is your discomfort around?
>
> FAMILY RESOURCE WORKER 1: I guess it's a personal discomfort, right? Because I really do think that everybody should breastfeed, so I try to put that aside because that is a judgment kind of thing and I don't want to make those judgments because there are all kinds of reasons why people don't breastfeed, and I get that. My other kind of discomfort around that is the World Health Organization code, right? I mean they

say – because I mean we've looked at what would we have to do to be that baby-friendly community. We do make sure we don't have any on site, but I always think about that whenever we buy formula. I think about what am I going to say if I am questioned by the [funders].

LESLEY: And are you saying that they would actually have a policy against it?

FAMILY RESOURCE WORKER 1: I don't know. I've never asked the question because I don't want to know the answer. If they did have a policy against it, then I would be in violation of that policy because I still do it, right? So, if I don't ask the question and I don't know, then there you go.

FAMILY RESOURCE WORKER 2: My discomfort around isn't so much that, because if I am going out and getting formula for somebody then they are not breastfeeding, so that whole thing is off the table anyway. They are not for a multitude of reasons, and that's not the discomfort for me. The discomfort for me is that I am buying this now, but what happens next month? This is an emergency but, first of all, why is it an emergency? And it's that inability to say, well, next month I can buy you formula on this date to get you through. So, there's an inconsistency about it, and there is desperation about it and that's what my discomfort is. I do feel uncomfortable going into Walmart and buying formula because that is where it is the cheapest and walking out and running into a pregnant woman coming in the other direction. But that is my personal discomfort in terms of breastfeeding policy and all that. I feel like stopping her and saying, "This isn't for me. You should breastfeed your baby." I do have that feeling, but generally the discomfort is around why do we have to do this, and you know, we can't continue it in any kind of consistent way because we can't do it for everybody, and we can't. It's the crisis around the lack of food for baby and for family, but for baby specifically at that time.

A health policy worker interviewed discussed concerns about the provincial breastfeeding policy:

> I do worry about the anxiety that the breastfeeding policy causes for the family resources centres, and they do all they can to provide that

> supportive environment for women to try to breastfeed ... Obviously, we would like to see supportive environments for women to choose that option, but within the breastfeeding policy, I don't think it is incongruent to look at the marketing by formula companies and corporations that benefit from ill health, and also be honest about what is really happening and ask: How do we support a women-centred harm-reduction model around infant food insecurity? How do we support women for them to try on breastfeeding? If they don't want to do it, how do we help them get access to the proper developmental formula? We need to do both. I think if the public health system is serious about going upstream, then they have to be able to hear that and to be honest about what is really happening. In order to have health equity we need to be honest, and us health equity types, we need to walk the talk. We need to be bold and we need to be brave, and we need to work together and we need to expose the stuff that is really happening, or the public health system will continue to think they are doing the right thing when in fact they are supporting a system that is more and more having to go underground.

While the Public Health Agency of Canada guide suggests that CPNP workers refer food insecure mothers to food banks for infant formula because they are "less directly tied to the protection, promotion and support of breastfeeding," a Nova Scotia food bank coordinator indicated that his organization was not free from local pressure over the provision of formula. He noted that there were no formal policies concerning infant formula distribution at his organization, or provincially that he knew of, other than to adhere to expiry dates.[15] He also asserted he had been told by someone (he did not know whom or by what authority) that mothers were "given certain grants at times from children's service to buy formula," and thus that providing formula might not be necessary.[16] The coordinator noted that he was advised by a hospital staff member (possibly a dietitian) about what to say or not say about formula, and agreed that it was not the food bank's job to recommend products, indicating that he was careful in his exchanges with mothers concerning formula. He suggested that people might have an issue with what he did if they thought the "breast was the best thing," but emphasized that was not for him to comment on *how* people feed babies.

Additionally, the food bank coordinator suggested that inconsistent availability of formula in food banks across the province was probably due to a lack of finances at certain sites and the nature of formula donation. He explained that occasionally formula was donated from the local grocery store, but noted that stores had a tendency to "hold onto the products because they are so pricey," choosing to mark them down rather than donate them. He further explained that stores throw out formula when it reaches the expiry date in order to protect themselves from liability over unsafe food. His organization didn't publicize that formula was available because it would not have been able to provide it to everyone in need, although it would place individual orders for pickup at the local drugstore to ensure that a client received the right type of formula. He described placing two or three orders for formula a week a couple of years earlier, spending $250 to $300 a month, which was difficult to sustain. Occasionally individuals brought formula to the food bank but it was often near its expiry. If someone wanted a donation that had expired on the same day, the food bank might distribute it, but normally it would be dumped in the compost.

Infact Canada, a national organization committed to protecting, promoting, and supporting breastfeeding, criticizes charity-provided formula at food banks as a violation of the *International Code of Marketing of Breast-Milk Substitutes* in that such free distribution is considered a form of marketing and therefore not baby friendly.[17] The code stipulates how to handle the distribution of donated and discounted formula, which is used as a marketing strategy by formula companies and has been found to negatively affect breastfeeding duration and exclusivity.[18] Additionally, the code stipulates, "Where donated supplies of infant formula or other products within the scope of this Code are distributed outside an institution, the institution or organization should take steps to ensure that supplies can be continued as long as the infants concerned need them."[19] This was precisely the dilemma that the family resource worker I interviewed described.

Infact Canada has also publicly denounced Food Banks Canada for its corporate partnership with the infant formula company Nestlé, which has been criticized for violating the code through direct marketing that offers women free samples.[20] Food Banks Canada responded with a statement, posted on Infact Canada's website, that it has never received formula donations from Nestlé for distribution but has applied Nestlé's financial donations to programming.

In Nova Scotia, policy enactors working for the provincial government were largely unaware of such debates about food charity for infants. For example, a policy worker from the Department of Community Services did not know that formula was inconsistently available from food banks. When I interviewed her, she was surprised to hear that anyone would have to pray to receive formula – but not that someone might have to steal it:

POLICY WORKER: So some food banks have formula and some don't?

LESLEY: Yes, food charity for babies was not anything mothers could rely on.

POLICY WORKER: It is like you have to pray it will be there.

LESLEY: Well, in some cases women actually did have to pray, literally.

POLICY WORKER: Oh, you mean *pray,* pray, really? Here in Nova Scotia? Wow, that's a new one.

LESLEY: And people had to steal as well.

POLICY WORKER: Yeah, 'cause they have to.

One health policy worker had little to say about charity formula provisioning other than her department had no formal relationship with food banks because they were community-based voluntary organizations. When I asked if there were any policies concerning formula in Nova Scotian food banks, she replied, "Probably not." Another health policy worker was unaware of the status of food charity for infants and asked me whether food banks stocked formula:

LESLEY: No, there are public asks for formula on many food bank websites across Canada, but some believe Canadians should rethink donating formula to food banks as it might create barriers to breastfeeding. For example, Infact Canada issued a press release in 2005 concerning this.

POLICY WORKER: You're kidding me. What right do they have to say that? But the food charity model, I hear horror stories from the family resource centres about, not just the inaccessible policies of those food banks but the attitudinal stuff is atrocious and the quality of the food.

> One family took home a can of dog food, because the label was off it. We have to get rid of [food banks because] they are socially divisive. It has been twenty years that I have been doing social justice type stuff, and we are going to hell in a handbasket because we don't give a shit about anybody any more. We have to get rid of those frigging food banks. We have to get people talking about this.

A different health policy worker was silent about whether food banks were violating the code in their inconsistent provisioning of formula, but program workers grappled with the incongruity between disdain for the food charity model and the implications for food insecure mothers and infants of failing to supply formula by this method. One worker expressed concern about the difficulty of ensuring supply at food banks, as this work fell to volunteers and organizations that did not have the resources to sustain it. When she received phone calls from mothers looking for formula, she always asked how much formula they had left. The answer was often, "Well, maybe enough for one bottle." At that point, she noted, "usually they have tried other avenues, but if there's not some facilitation around getting formula, I'm thinking, what would they have done in that case? … That's definitely a situation where that baby is not food secure at all. There's not even an inkling of food security when it's all balancing on one bottle."

She also explained that she did not have an issue with formula being supplied by food banks but with random donations that led to babies being fed different types of formula:

> Another food insecurity issue is the switching from one formula to the next because … parents are not able to access the acceptable one. See, that for me is also food insecurity, if they aren't able to access the same one it can cause problems with digestion. Then they can end up at the doctor and the doctor says, "Oh well, this is what the issue is. It's the formula and they are allergic and they can't have that." And, then they end up going on some other formula which is generally more expensive. So, then you are in another whole kettle of fish.

Another program worker thought that food charity in general was a failed model for dealing with food insecurity, but that as the only channel available it needed to better address the needs of families with infants in need of formula:

> I have an issue with food banks in general, but if we are going to have food banks for families – even though it was supposed to be a temporary measure twenty-five years ago, and now it is a big business – then let's service the whole family and let's have infant formula and not just one brand. They have emergency food banks for pets. You can get food for a dog or a cat, but they don't have infant formula at a food bank?

The fact that community-based organizations must deal directly with the outcomes of infant food insecurity is unsurprising. Rather than implementing public programs directly, neo-liberal social welfare reform is typified by governments steering approaches to policy implementation within the non-profit sector in order to deliver key social welfare programs such as child welfare, early parenting support, and child care. There has also been an increase since the 1980s in voluntary associations and faith-based organizations that provide basic social services to the poor, as illustrated by the rise of food banks in Canada, and other high-income countries as a response to food insecurity.[21]

I conducted research in 2016 with CPNP projects and food banks across Canada to assess the dynamics of formula access from such organizations beyond Nova Scotia.[22] I explored typical organizational responses to infant formula needs, availability, and distribution practices, and examined how these were shaped by formal and informal policies and values. This research showed that CPNP projects were routinely approached for such support. Three typical organizational responses were common: strict adherence to baby-friendly directives and a refusal to supply emergency formula; covert provision of formula (described as a mother-centred approach) while notionally upholding formal baby-friendly policy; and a combination of feminist food justice approaches and a baby-friendly policy (a baby's right to food and a mother's right to feed), realized through efforts to find non-CPNP funding to provide infant formula consistently (Figure 1).

The CPNP projects in this sample most frequently chose to offer covert support. On the one hand, feminist values support breastfeeding. On the other, the same values drive a commitment to help all mothers regardless

FIGURE 1
Continuum of CPNP organizational responses to formula needs

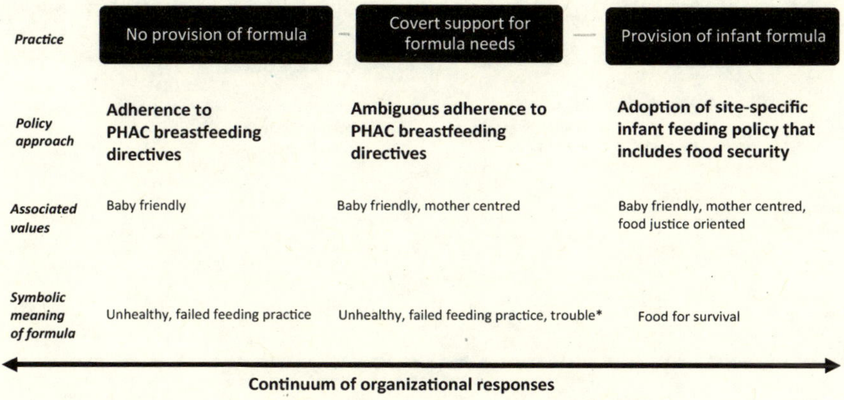

* Some expressed experiencing "trouble" or criticism from other organizations when it became known they had provided formula, and others worried about getting into trouble with funders if they used project funds to purchase formula.

Adapted from Lesley Frank, "Finding Formula: Community-Based Organizational Responses to Infant Formula Needs Due to Household Food Insecurity," *Canadian Food Studies Journal* 5, 1 (2018): 90–112.

of how they fed their babies, recognizing the challenges they confront: poverty, desperation over their responsibility to feed, and shame in foraging for formula. Nonetheless, feminist values were pushed underground because of contentious and what some family resource workers perceived as class-blind infant feeding politics.

My research found a similar spectrum of organizational responses in food banks across the country: never providing infant formula (either because staff did not feel knowledgeable about the specialty food needs of infants or because of baby-friendly positions); sometimes providing formula, but of random types and only if it was donated; always providing formula but of unpredictable types; or always providing purchased, rather than donated, formula of the type needed because the food bank operated a specialized infant charity program (see Figure 2). These responses were shaped less by breastfeeding policy than by charity ideology or a food justice orientation. Only one food bank indicated that its work aligned with feminist values, even though mothers were the clients who showed up at food bank doors most often.[23] The diversity of responses demonstrates

FIGURE 2

Continuum of food bank organizational responses to formula needs

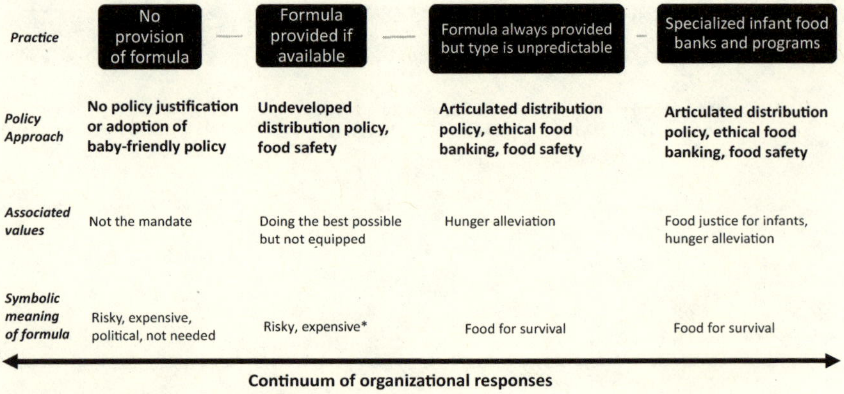

* Some interviewees felt that there was a health risk to infants, due to a lack of skills and knowledge about infant formula among food bank workers.

Adapted from Lesley Frank, "Finding Formula: Community-Based Organizational Responses to Infant Formula Needs Due to Household Food Insecurity," *Canadian Food Studies Journal* 5, 1 (2018): 90–112.

the inability of food banks to respond to the problem even though the PHAC guidelines identify them as an avenue of referral for food insecure mothers. The research also calls into question ethical food banking practice, as the ethics code of Food Banks Canada stipulates that food banks will "provide food and other assistance to those needing help regardless of race, national or ethnic origin, citizenship, colour, religion, sex, sexual orientation, income source, *age*, or mental or physical ability."[24]

The stories of mothers who do not breastfeed in conditions of poverty, as well as the experiences of policy and program workers tasked with supporting family and infant well-being, demonstrate the urgent need to develop public policy on issues of infant food insecurity related to formula affordability and access. Statistics on breastfeeding duration suggest that in Canada today, an infant's access to breast milk – as the "best" and "only" food given to infants in the first six months of life – is insecure, as exclusive breastfeeding is largely *not* sustainable.

Nevertheless, not breastfeeding or stopping breastfeeding early does not mean a denial of food for most infants. Across all income groups, mothers commonly feed their babies formula as a breast milk alternative that is considered an acceptable food product and for which Health Canada provides feeding recommendations.[25] For low-income mothers, however, breast milk alternatives can be unaffordable and inaccessible, causing serious problems of food access and nutritional deprivation. Current Canadian policy fails to address problems of access to breast milk alternatives for low-income mothers (except for those receiving provincial income assistance if they require medically indicated formulas), even though international, national, and provincial policy – by endorsing the *International Code of Marketing of Breast-Milk Substitutes* – upholds the concept that such food products should be made accessible to those who need them. As the code *itself* recognizes,

> There is a legitimate market for infant formula and for suitable ingredients from which to prepare it; that all these products should accordingly be made accessible to those who need them through commercial or non-commercial distribution systems; and that they should not be marketed or distributed in ways that may interfere with the protection and promotion of breastfeeding ... [Institutions and organizations that distribute donated formula should] take steps to ensure that supplies can be continued as long as the infants concerned need them.[26]

When there is no state support for emergency infant food, leaving mothers to turn to community services that admittedly are ill equipped to respond, is it not time for serious discussion and action within policy realms to address optimal formula feeding within food insecure families? How do we provide support that ensures babies are adequately fed, using acceptable methods, targeting both those who breastfeed (which should include adequate nutrition for mothers) *and* those who do not? Is community-level food justice work to ensure that the food insecure infant receives food not a clearer interpretation of the international code? The fact that food insecure mothers encounter a commercial system they cannot afford, and that there is no adequate non-commercial distribution system, demonstrates that this is an aspect of the code we have ignored in Canada. Furthermore, women must engage with the latter system despite facing resistance from those who conceptualize any free distribution of formula (even through "normal procurement channels" in line with the code) as harmful to the promotion and protection of breastfeeding. Improving breastfeeding success need not involve food deprivation for the youngest and most vulnerable Canadians. It is time to rethink infant feeding policy at the level of practice in light of food insecurity, taking as a guide a position that ensures food first for mothers and infants.

More important, however, is to consider whether emergency food systems are the best way to address food justice. While community-based services and resources do much to support mothers in the daily struggle of feeding the baby, food charity offerings do not make for sound infant feeding practice or for food justice. This problem cannot be solved, only mitigated, by community organizations that are at the end-point of policy failure. Mothers seek help from food banks and family resource centres to feed their babies largely because state supports for early parenting are inadequate. Addressing infant food insecurity through community-based food charity models throughout Canada does not create the economic security or social conditions necessary for successful breastfeeding or formula feeding. Charity is not food justice.

Some organizations have developed somewhat better systems, but upstream approaches – those emanating from federal and provincial jurisdictions – are better suited to address the many structural barriers to both types of feeding. Failing to make those upstream policy shifts will continue to obscure the serious problems of unequal food access, potential food risk, and food injustice that mothers and infants experience when women are forced into pathologized foraging for formula. As Canadian anthropologist Penny Van Esterik argues, food insecurity and infant feeding problems are a feminist right-to-food issue, involving the intersecting rights of mother and infant: the right to food, the right to feed, and the right to be fed.[27]

Conclusion

IMPLICATIONS FOR RESEARCH, POLICY, AND PRACTICE

The research presented here explored how infant feeding practices – those related to food production, food acquisition, modes of feeding, and what is consumed – are shaped by household food insecurity. The results add to our understanding of the social relations of family food insecurity in high-income countries. The mothers I interviewed were the people primarily responsible for feeding their infants within constrained economic circumstances. They expressed feelings of failed mothering characterized by an inconsistent ability to provide desirable food through acceptable channels, against a backdrop of contested ideas and policy positions about optimal feeding. For many, *how* they fed their babies was trumped by the fear of being unable to do so at all.

This research contributes to scholarship concerning the social, rather than nutritional, relations of infant feeding in low-income families by providing evidence of how household and maternal food insecurity is a determinant of food production, acquisition, and infant food consumption. It identifies structural factors that affect family food practice and negative nutritional outcomes (which include the infant in complex intra-household social relations) as serious matters of health inequity. For the women I interviewed, household food insecurity led to a high breastfeeding initiation rate, yet it also compromised maternal food consumption and breastfeeding success. Some mothers, however, continued to breastfeed despite being food insecure. Further exploration is needed for us to understand why that was so, but the stories here suggest that a positive disposition toward breastfeeding, strong breastfeeding support, and personal strategies for dealing with household food insecurity (making sure mothers eat, delaying bill payment to buy healthy food) contributed to success despite structural barriers.

Statistics on exclusive breastfeeding in Canada also indicate that cultural factors are relevant: Asian women, women of colour, and women who have immigrated to Canada within the last five years have higher rates of breastfeeding initiation and exclusive breastfeeding than white women (the category that includes 85 percent of mothers in this study).[1] While breastfeeding trends appear to differ among cultural/racial groups, the ways in which income and cultural/racial identities come together to shape infant feeding practice in Canada are not well understood.[2] Social context also matters. As barriers to breastfeeding continuation and duration, poverty and food insecurity are intertwined with other factors: cultural and family history, social environment, and available support. Infant feeding, like all food practice, embodies complex social relations that are both enmeshed with and situated beyond issues related to poverty.

The stories here also suggest that the severity of household food insecurity affects breastfeeding success. Some mothers' experience of food insecurity varied from more to less extreme over time. For a few, breastfeeding success occurred only when there was a second earner in the household. The women with the highest levels of maternal food insecurity (those who stole food, ate food scraps, pawned their belongings for food, habitually received food charity, or went without food completely) tended not to breastfeed or stopped very early. Thus, the relationship between severity of food insecurity and breastfeeding duration merits attention, particularly across different cultural groups, in light of increasing rates of household and individual food insecurity in Canada and the tendency of mothers to compromise their own food intake to feed their children.

This research also contributes to our understanding of the food insecurity of formula-fed infants in high-income countries. When breastfeeding is compromised in food insecure homes, infant food insecurity results from the non-affordability of formula; the failed charity model of formula provisioning in Canada; and the health risks associated with expired formula, habitual switching of formula brands, and inappropriate food consumption. This is a serious nutrition equity issue that requires national attention: the elephant in the room that we need to make visible so we can discuss it at the policy and practice level. The elephant, so to speak, is there partly because of historical tension between supporting breastfeeding and making formula more readily available. Formula availability has affected breastfeeding success worldwide, and improperly prepared infant formula has been at the root of severe malnutrition and infant mortality, spurring necessary policy to regulate its marketing.[3] But when food insecurity is a barrier to lactation, making formula inaccessible in order to protect breastfeeding is essentially throwing out the baby with the bathwater.

It is crucial that mothers' complex experiences of infant food insecurity be more fully recognized and integrated into policy debates. And mothers are not the only people we need to hear from. While the responsibilities of family food work fall disproportionally to them, and solely to them in the case of breastfeeding, they are not the only ones involved. Asking only mothers about infant feeding perpetuates their position as having primary responsibility and ignores the practices of other food insecure primary feeders or co-feeders who have no access to breast milk: grandparents and other family caregivers, foster parents, single fathers, fathers within either same-sex or heterosexual couples.

The mothers' stories identified problems of food insecurity that were specific to their infants: worry about being able to produce food via breastfeeding, running out of formula because of inadequate income, needing to rely on unacceptable food acquisition methods and questionable food products obtained through charity routes, and sub-optimal food consumption. Canadian infant feeding policy has not addressed these problems. Nor has food security policy articulated, or income security policy adequately addressed, the food needs of low-income mothers and infants. Thus, both breastfeeding and optimal formula feeding are problematic, and early nutrition conditions for infants – essential to their ability to thrive in a host of important areas throughout their lives – are at risk. Infant food security can exist only when infants, their families, and most importantly their mothers have affordable access to food at all times. This depends on economic, nutritional, social, and cultural support of mothers in their work as producers of food through breastfeeding, and access to reliable, safe, affordable, and personally acceptable alternatives when breastfeeding is not possible – for whatever reason.

The mothers' stories also pointed to key policy areas shaping their experiences. To be clear, there is *no* infant food security policy in Canada, but mothers and policy and program staff provided insight into how formal and informal policy shapes their lives and their work. Public policy is a primary function of the state in advanced capitalist societies, guiding intervention in a wide range of social issues, such as education, health, housing, and income security.[4] Under Danish sociologist Gøsta Esping-Anderson's classification system of welfare states, Canada is considered liberal, meaning that it tends to target social benefits to the poor and to expect most individuals to support themselves and their families through the labour market.[5]

This neo-liberal orientation plays out in how we access food. Food is mostly a commodity, and families obtain it primarily through their wages. Food work occurs within the family as a private matter despite its important contribution to the social reproduction of the state. Intervention in household food shortage occurs only for those most in need, with a noticeable shift from state support to charity-based support over the past thirty years. Additionally, food choice is shaped by sanctioned and promoted state claims about what is "good to eat" and, in the case of babies, also how they should be fed. Proper attention to infant nutrition is positioned as a moral imperative for mothers, or what Michel Foucault termed a *biological-moral* responsibility, whereby children's proper nutrition becomes a problem of motherhood and an internalized moral obligation.[6]

It is no surprise that there is no *infant* food security policy, not only because infant food insecurity suffers from invisibility but also because Canada, and Nova Scotia specifically, has little in the way of food security policy at all. The mothers and policy and program workers I interviewed identified intersecting policy domains that have a role to play, but the responsibility to solve the problem does not belong to any of them. The Nova Scotia government endorses food charity as the solution, as evidenced by a 2016 announcement of non-refundable tax credits to farmers for food bank donations.[7] As Graham Riches argues in *Food Bank Nations,* the role of government is not to endorse food charity; it is to fulfill the human right to adequate food.[8]

There was convergence between what mothers and policy enactors/ program workers had to say about the effect of public policy on the lives of families. They agreed that adequate income security is essential to support mothers in the work of feeding their babies, pointing to income-based solutions to infant food insecurity. Additionally, they recognized a lack of other institutional and cultural supports for the work of breastfeeding, and for social reproduction caring work in general. Policy conversations about feeding practices other than breastfeeding were more contentious, as some policy enactors were uncomfortable talking about infant formula, especially about making formula more accessible to food insecure mothers. Others, when hearing about the negative outcomes of charity-based formula acquisition, expressed concern about a lack of state support for optimal formula feeding in low-income populations.

One health policy worker called for a harm reduction approach at the practice level, recognizing that food insecure babies need to be fed as a matter of social justice and of gender equity for mothers left responsible when they are least economically secure. She pointed to the discrepancy between government policy stipulating that all new programs and policies require gender analysis and the lack of state support for infant food security and the work of feeding a baby:

> [Infant food insecurity] is a gender issue for me mainly. It is a continued social norm that it is women's domain to take care of infants. At what point do children become society's responsibility? At what point? At what age? We don't have a societal responsibility for life at the beginning; it is women's responsibility, and it is up to them to fend for themselves and to figure it out regardless of their circumstance, and in fact you are financially penalized when you do get pregnant. Yet a couple of years ago, we were told [within the federal government that] any new programs should be going through a sex- and gender-based analysis. There is a lot of incongruence; it is really mind boggling.

This worker articulated a central problem surrounding nutrition equity for infants: that feeding a baby has been construed as the individualized work of motherhood, not a social problem in need of social solutions and state support. She stressed that family and infant food insecurity is a result of external, systemic relations of poverty and gender inequality, despite its construction as a mothering issue.

When asked what kind of policies are needed to build food security, one family resource worker identified government income redistribution mechanisms and a reframing of the work of feeding children that does not position it as individualized women's work:

> A guaranteed annual income and an increase in the child tax credit so that it really does adequately reflect what it costs to raise children. This is a gender issue, too. Who are the ones who are poor? Women. I am fairly confident that if it were men that were primarily responsible for feeding children that we wouldn't even be talking about this.

One health policy worker expressed extreme weariness about working within a system that does not respond to the social problems of poverty and gender inequality (which she saw at the root of infant food insecurity), finding her biggest challenge in not allowing herself to be immobilized by frustration. She also found a social disconnection between civil servants and those living in poverty, which she attributed to lack of awareness about day-to-day realities and the practical effects of public policy, as well as to philosophical differences over ways to address the issue. She thought her role was to listen and to give anecdotal evidence to civil servants to bridge this gap:[9]

> The biggest thing is health practitioners just don't know to address poverty as a determinant of health; they don't know what is happening and they can't empathize. I believe so strongly in trying to lessen that social disconnect. Policy is politically driven most of the time, but it is people making policy, and if people had greater empathy and really care, really understood the issues and how it impacts people, that would help … I learn about most of the policies impacting the families that we are talking about through my community friends and even just talking to you. Then what I try to do … is talk to other civil servants, because we need to be enraged about some of these policies. For those that can be moved, we need to keep telling stories, giving examples, and we need to keep solidarity among those that care about equity.

I agree with her that infant food insecurity is not well understood within policy domains, and that there is a lack of policy response, or ineffective policy response, to the problem. As a result, individual families, primarily mothers, continue to deal with the issue on their own and/or with the support of under-resourced community services. The social problem is framed as a feeding issue, not a poverty issue, and solutions are targeted at changing mothers' behaviour. This is despite the fact that the UN *Convention on the Rights of the Child,* to which Canada is a signatory, recognizes poverty as a barrier to child rights and outlines state responsibility for child survival and development rights: the right to an adequate standard of living, particularly in regard to food, clothing, and housing. Additionally, international breastfeeding policy – including the *International Code of Marketing of Breast-Milk Substitutes,* the *Baby-Friendly Hospital Initiative,* and the *Innocenti Declaration: On the Protection, Promotion and Support of Breastfeeding* – explicitly states that optimal infant feeding and nutrition cannot be divorced from the health and nutrition of mothers and wider social and economic barriers to breastfeeding.

Clearly, infant food insecurity is a result of a succession of public policy failures. First and foremost, Canada has weak income security policies and programs during maternity and inadequate income-related protection and practical support for the work of infant feeding. This results in high rates of household food insecurity that disproportionally affects families with young children. The situation leads to compromised breastfeeding, difficulty in affording infant formula, and ultimately ineffective, at times dangerous, charity-based community responses that place a heavy burden on all those caught by debates about *how* babies should be fed while they navigate the challenges of feeding them at all.

A much broader set of solutions is necessary. Canadian policy domains related to food production, food access, and sustainable food systems have all but ignored the special case of infant feeding and infant food. Food security policy recognizes that economic security is essential for food access, yet it fails to acknowledge the structural constraints on breastfeeding and problems of access to infant formula in low-income circumstances. The problem cannot be solved by breastfeeding policy alone, or even by more inclusive infant feeding policy that considers the non-breastfed infant. The bottom line is that infants have a right to food and mothers have a right to feed them, but it is not only the mother's responsibility to do so.

Article 27 of the UN *Convention on the Rights of the Child* stipulates, "Children have the right to a standard of living that is good enough to meet their physical and mental needs. Governments should help families and guardians who cannot afford to provide this, particularly with regard to food, clothing and housing."[10] The stories told in this work illuminate a failed social contract between Canadian governments and Canadian families in the public good of raising society's next generation of healthy children.

At a structural level, social security is necessary to establish the conditions that facilitate optimal infant feeding practices. Building infant food security means ensuring the right to a level of income security that enables families to perform the labour of feeding and to cover the costs associated with either lactation or formula feeding. It also means the right to maternity protection: legally assured and income-protected leave from paid work; and for those receiving welfare benefits, protection from the requirement to seek paid work. Protected *parental* leave means that not only mothers are encompassed by this policy.

Currently, not everyone in Canada has access to such protection, as families are not always eligible to receive benefits through existing mechanisms such as federal maternity/parental leave. In fact, for the mothers interviewed in this work, federal maternity/parental benefits were almost non-existent. We also know that families relying on provincial income assistance in Nova Scotia are hundreds of dollars short monthly from the capacity to afford a basic nutritious diet.[11] And low-wage earners, particularly minimum-wage earners, are not able to bring in an income sufficient for household food security. Government income-tested tax transfers such as federal and provincial child benefits have helped to bridge the gap, serving as a guaranteed annual income for Canadian families, but the amount that is guaranteed varies across the country due to differences in provincial credits.[12] Some provinces provide tax transfers targeted to maternity and early childhood. (Newfoundland and Labrador's Mother Baby Nutrition Supplement and New Brunswick's Prenatal Benefit Program and Postnatal Benefit Program are examples.) We have yet to evaluate their effectiveness, however, when it comes to structurally supporting the nutritional needs of maternity and early childhood.

It is good news that we now have a federal poverty reduction strategy that includes the goal of reducing child poverty, albeit only cutting it in half by 2030. Recent Statistics Canada data confirms the effectiveness of the Canada Child Benefit in reducing child poverty.[13] Unfortunately, Nova Scotia bucks the trend, being the only province to show an increase in child poverty since 2015. This demonstrates the urgency of coordinating federal and provincial poverty reduction efforts, heightening poverty eradication goals, and carefully monitoring all interventions – particularly in early childhood, the period of life with highest rate of poverty in Canada and when poverty has its greatest health impact.[14] Both federal and provincial governments are accountable for meeting their human rights obligations to provide social security for families and children: the right to income security to procure basic needs and services, and the right to adequate food for infants and young children through maternal and child protection.

Optimal infant feeding practices are nutritionally sound, affordable, safe, culturally appropriate, just, and supported, and that depends on social security. Optimal practices also ensure infants' *individual* food security, through either breastfeeding or accessible, affordable, and nutritionally sound alternatives. The stories here show that enabling sound infant feeding practices goes beyond income and food security. Mothers and community program workers stressed that caring and feeding work needs practical resources, such as breastfeeding support in hospital, distribution of relevant information, and hands-on help from lactation consultants, public health home visitors, and community-based family resource staff. They also emphasized the need for community and institutional support for public breastfeeding or for not breastfeeding. Their stories highlighted a lack of information for mothers who use formula, and the serious oversight of leaving access to affordable formula to charity instead of making it a matter of public policy. Building infant food security means enhancing these practical institutional and community supports to form an integral component of health and social services for families. Doing so will help us to fulfil our collective responsibility for the welfare of children and the social reproduction of society.

It is time to remind readers of my initial reason for conducting this study and writing this book. It is my long answer to the breastfeeding paradox: to say more than "It's complicated" to the question of why food insecure mothers do not breastfeed more. The mothers I interviewed made me think critically about the extent to which different feeding practices (or food substances) are really the issue. Political scientist George Kent argues that we must focus on the *social conditions* that facilitate what he refers to as "sound child feeding practices."[15] These mothers' stories provide insight into the social conditions at play and urge us to move beyond thinking merely about infant feeding interventions at the individual level. We need to consider how to implement broader policy goals for economic, social, and food justice. If food is truly a right, a notion that Canada has endorsed through international agreements, then social policy must be expanded to realize the right to breastfeed. This must include protections within labour policy, institutions, and public settings, and more essentially, through adequate income, food security, and maternal nutrition. Broader policy considerations are also necessary to support food insecure mothers when breastfeeding is not possible. Food insecurity is about poverty, and it is poverty that makes households and mothers food insecure. It is also poverty that makes infants food insecure – regardless of how they are fed.

Appendix

ANATOMY OF THE STUDY

Why? Conceptual Tools

What is the relationship between household food insecurity and infant feeding practice? What role, if any, does Canadian public policy play in this relationship? These are the guiding research questions of the sociological case study presented in this book. The text also draws from a research project conducted in 2016–17 on infant formula availability and distribution practices, and on the formal and informal policies and values that influence whether and how formula is made available to food insecure mothers (and, at times, other caregivers) throughout Canada.[1]

The research is both critical and integrative. Critical research aims to expose oppression and create possibilities for social change.[2] It asks critical questions about the nature of society and the status quo. Investigation using this lens reveals that infant feeding practice occurs within social and family relations of feeding and eating that are typical of gendered divisions of labour, yet varies considerably among different groups of people. Integrative research on social relations upholds the idea that social phenomena are best understood by exploring the interaction between micro-level experiences and objective social structures.

Theoretical debate about the exact nature of the relationship between the individual and society is at the heart of the discipline of sociology. Referred to as the structure–agency debate, or the dialectic of individual and society, the question has a long history through the work of social and sociological theorists. Like many others, I view the relationship between experience and structure as a *process*. I do not see it as determinist, whereby structure *causes* experiences to occur in universal ways. The relationship is cyclical or, more aptly, simultaneous: structure shapes or influences experience, while experience reinforces existing structure or has the power to shift or change structure.

I have adopted a social relations approach as a means of integrating experience (feeding practice) and structures (of which policy is one component). Social relations are the relations between people and wider social structures that form the basis of social structure. The concept of social relations – which sociologist Blake Poland and his colleagues unpack as the "social structure such as class, race, and gender; institutional practices, collective and individual behaviors, and intersecting personal biographies" – can help us to understand any social context.[3] In the context of food and eating, Treena Delormier, Katherine Frohlich, and Louise Potvin argue that the concept of social relations is a basis for understanding that bridges symbolic and cultural meanings with materialist orientations focusing on social, political, and economic factors.[4]

A social relations approach can also be used to explore the intersection of public policy (supported or shaped by other structural factors) and feeding practice by situating an inquiry within two realms: the everyday micro-level of individual experience and perception, and the world of documents and rules. I view the connections between public policy and experience in several key ways. First, as a component of government and organizational structures, policy – or its lack – shapes the social conditions under which we live. Second, public policies are expressions of perceived social needs; they are created, enforced, and changed according to conceptions of the best way to achieve societal goals. Third, public policy is ideological, and addresses certain goals in particular ways. For example, it can be an aspect of structures of inequality, reinforcing societal arrangements that benefit some at the expense of many. Finally, while it appears to be part of an objective institutional world, public policy is a product of human action. It originates at the micro-level of society and is shaped by cultural norms: the beliefs we hold and values we live by, particularly dominant values held by the privileged. Policy is also created and enforced within the day-to-day working lives of policy enactors, leaving it open to interpretation and subject to various degrees of compliance.

Because policy has, and is shaped by, these complex factors, studying the intersection of the social relations of infant feeding practices and food insecurity *and* public policy requires not only attention to written and unwritten policies (and the systems that support them) but also an in-depth understanding of a range of experiences and perceptions. Such an integrative approach to research has the potential to reveal the complexity of the social world. Additionally, positioning the research within an overall critical stance means that the results can serve as an advocacy tool for marginalized groups, creating the possibility for progressive change on social justice issues.

Infant food insecurity is a manifestation of multiple levels of social relations, as Figure 3 illustrates. The everyday activities of feeding infants and dealing with food insecurity within a household are *social practices:* what Alan Warde, in *The Practice of Eating,* refers to as "the fundamental units of social existence and hence the core concept of social analysis."[5] The infant's vulnerability over food access, lack of food, or poor-quality food due to financial constraint is realized through the effects of poverty and food insecurity on the everyday practice of feeding. The social practice of infant feeding entails social relationships between the eater and the feeder involving milk production, acquiring food through market and non-market sources, and the act of feeding and eating. These practices embody *social conditions,* illustrated within the middle ring of poverty and food insecurity in Figure 3. These are in turn embodiments of broader *socio-cultural relations* (gendered, racial, ethnocultural, geo-cultural) and *political-economic relations* (economic-material, policy related), represented by the outer ring of the figure.

Social relations do not occur in only one direction. As represented by the embedded spheres of Figure 3, wider structural factors shape social conditions and social practice, but the reverse occurs as well. For example, while the social practice of breastfeeding can create conditions of food security, the opposite also occurs, as the condition of food insecurity can shape infant feeding outcomes. My research explored precisely how the social practices involved in infant feeding, the social conditions of poverty and food security, and the wider cultural, political, and economic forces at play are connected. This framework informed the case study research design, the selection of the interview questions, and the analysis of data.

FIGURE 3
The social relations of infant food insecurity

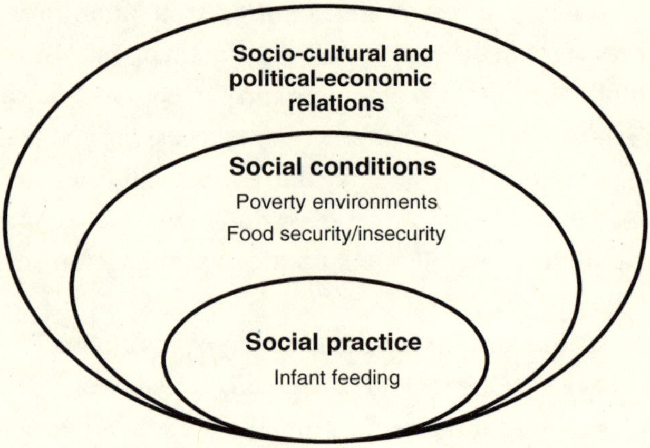

How? Methods and Organization

I used a three-phased qualitative case study to explore how infant feeding was affected by food insecurity in Nova Scotia.[6] Qualitative research is concerned with interpreting the meaning (the "why") and actions (the "how") of individuals according to their own subjective frames of reference, and case studies enable us to understand complex social phenomena within a real-life context.[7] Infant feeding and experiences of food insecurity take place primarily in the social spaces of families, and only qualitative inquiry can adequately interpret the "why" and "how" of such experiences.

Nova Scotia, the second-smallest province in Canada and with a largely rural population, is the overall unit of analysis of this study. My background in local community development work gave me established networks that offered enthusiastic support for the project, easing the recruitment issues that often occur with vulnerable populations. Family resource centre staff facilitated participation through in-kind transportation and child care.

Apart from logistics, however, Nova Scotia was ideal for the case study conceptually because the rate of breastfeeding initiation and exclusive breastfeeding to six months (markers of meeting provincial infant feeding recommendations) is lower than the national average, and Nova Scotia has the highest level of food insecurity of all Canadian provinces.[8] Detailed exploration of the Nova Scotian context opens the door to comparison with other cases, in different jurisdictions and with different dynamics.

Phase 1: Listening to Mothers

Phase 1 used qualitative interviews to explore mothers' experiences of infant feeding and household food insecurity. It involved twenty in-depth, face-to-face interviews with mothers who had at least one child between the ages of six months and two years living in food insecure homes. The interview questions were as follows:

1. How would you describe your relationship to food?

   Prompt: What is the significance of food in your house?
2. I'd like to hear about your experiences in feeding your baby/ies. Can you tell me about any plans you might have had in this regard before your baby was born?

   Prompt: What do you think may have influenced your plans?
3. What was feeding your baby like?

   Prompts: What method did you use, or combination of methods? What exactly did/do you feed your baby? Tell me about any difficulties and successes you have had concerning feeding your baby.
4. If how or what you fed your baby changed along the way, what brought those changes about?
5. Tell me about times you have felt food insecure, if any.

   Prompt: What circumstances shaped this feeling?
6. Now, what about your family? Was or is their experience of food security different from yours?

   Prompt: How is food security different or the same for your baby as it is for you? Can you tell me about any difficulties you've had in feeding your baby that are different from those you experience in feeding yourself or the rest of your family?
7. I'm interested in knowing about any connections between how and what you fed/feed your baby and living in low-income circumstances. Can you tell me about any connections?
8. Can you tell me about any strategies you use to secure food for your baby?

9. I'd like to talk about how policy might influence how and what you feed your baby. Policies are laws, rules, or guidelines by organizations such as the food bank, your workplace, or government departments or offices. They can cover issues such as how long your lunch break is, income assistance plans, and minimum wage rates. Can you think of any ways that such policies shape your decisions about feeding your baby?
10. Can you think of anything that would help make families' and their babies' food sources and supply secure?

Interview participants were selected in collaboration with Canada Prenatal Nutrition Program (CPNP) and Community Action Program for Children (CAPC) projects. Nova Scotia has eight CPNP and fourteen CAPC projects, most operating in conjunction with each other under the umbrella of a family resource centre. CPNP and CAPC projects function throughout Canada; they are community based and federally funded by the Public Health Agency of Canada. The goals of the CPNP are to reduce the incidence of unhealthy birth weights, improve the health of infants and mothers, and encourage breastfeeding. CAPC projects offer support to families with children from birth to age six facing challenging circumstances. The directors at all the family resource centres offering these programs were contacted, and eight agreed to recruit mothers for the study. The inclusion criteria were having had a baby in the last two years and having experienced food insecurity, regardless of infant feeding method. Either the mothers contacted me directly or I contacted them after staff confirmed their consent.

The interviews took place between February and May 2011 in twelve communities across Nova Scotia. Fifteen of the twenty interviews occurred at family resource centres and five took place in the homes of the interviewees by their request. Written informed consent was obtained beforehand, and all interviews were one to two hours long and were digitally recorded.

I used QSR International NVivo 9.2 qualitative-analysis software to aid in inductive analysis, and followed a three-step coding process. Initially transcripts were read on screen as open coding was conducted line by line to identify codes that relate to the topics of infant feeding and food insecurity very broadly. In other words, the codes were not predetermined, allowing interpretation to emerge from the data in a process of creating grounded theory.[9] After each interview had been analyzed using open coding, I made connections between the open codes in order to reduce the number of overarching categories. These categories were used for a re-coding of the transcripts. Finally, the data grouped by these category headings was further reduced and sorted by the three broad themes that form the structure of this book: breastfeeding as a food security measure, breastfeeding as an insecure food system, and infant food insecurity related to formula feeding. These themes together form a typology of infant feeding experiences in food insecure households and are explored in turn in Chapters 2, 3, and 4 of the current work. The effects of public policy on mothers' lives emerged as a categorical sub-theme of each these major themes and was the focus of Phase 2 of the study.

Phase 2: Developing a Policy Review

I began Phase 2 by mapping mothers' responses to being asked how policy shaped what they fed their babies and by what method, and what could help or hinder food security for their babies and their families. I then organized the data into four main sub-categories of policy that mothers thought were essential for infant food security:

- Family policies and programs
- Infant feeding/food policy and programs
- Alternative food acquisition
- Income security

This process served as a scan of the policy environment in Nova Scotia, and in some other provinces for comparative purposes. It also encompassed relevant national policies and programs affecting Nova Scotia, as well as wider international agreements in the key areas of infant feeding and food security.

I then organized a variety of identified policy documents under the categories, and analyzed each one for evidence of a link between infant feeding and the condition of food insecurity, noting if the policy had the potential to support food security or lead to food insecurity for infants. I included not only the policies that interviewees had mentioned during

Phase 1 but also broader policy documents that they were unaware of and therefore did not discuss. All these policy sources – community, provincial (Nova Scotia and beyond), national, and international (in the form of international agreements to which Canada is a signatory) were included in the resulting policy review.

The review then served as a tool for discussion and reflection during interviews with government and community program workers.

Phase 3: Speaking with Policy and Program Workers

Phase 3 further explored the relationship between infant feeding and food insecurity by developing a third source of data: interviews with government and community organization staff who had direct knowledge of the policy areas reviewed in Phase 2. The experiences and perceptions of policy and program workers were important because policy is often informally created and/or enforced within the day-to-day working lives of policy enactors. As well, formalized policy is left open to interpretation and to various levels of compliance in the field.

In July and August 2011, I conducted five semi-structured in-person interviews with six workers known to have expertise in the four main policy areas identified by mothers. In one instance, two people participated in the interview at the request of the organization. Four interviews took place at the workplaces of the interviewees, and one took place at a home office. The interviewees represented health and community services government departments and community organizations focused on food security, infant feeding, and family resources.

My requests for interviews with representatives of the provincial food bank organization and a national organization committed to breastfeeding promotion and protection were turned down. A request for a formal interview with the federal Department of Agriculture and Agri-food (which was responsible for monitoring the implementation of *Canada's Action Plan for Food Security*) was also denied, as the contact person deemed that my interests were really a matter of infant feeding policy. Somewhat ironically, this perception proved my claim that there is little conceptualization of infant feeding practice as a food security issue. Although I was not able to conduct a formal interview, two departmental employees provided information about the status of the *Action Plan* by way of a conference call.

The in-person interviews lasted one to two hours. Using the policy review document developed in Phase 2 enabled me to collect data on the subjective meanings that staff attached to policy intent, the experience of enacting policy, and their perceptions of the relationship between infant feeding and food insecurity, based on the following questions:

1. To what extent have you had a chance to look over the policy review? (If the interviewee has not done so, the researcher presents the document briefly.)
2. Tell me your thoughts on this review in general.
3. Tell me in your own words what you think the policy you are most familiar with is trying to accomplish.

   Prompt: To your knowledge, what is the history of this policy?
4. I'm interested in how policies do or don't shape experiences of infant food security. Do you have any ideas about the effect of (specific policy) on infant food security?

   Prompt: Does the policy support optimal feeding?
5. Can you describe any challenges this policy creates for women in feeding their babies?
6. Do you have any opinions about how government or public institutional policy could better support infant food security?

Phase 3 interviews were transcribed and a work-related pseudonym assigned to each interviewee to provide anonymity while identifying the general area of expertise and level of responsibility. I then conducted a thematic analysis using a process of comparing and contrasting data from the parent interviews and data from the policy enactor interviews.

Convergence and Contradictions

The final stage of analysis explored points of convergence and contradiction within the three phases of the case study. My intention was to synthesize the data sources to build a comprehensive picture of the complex relationship between infant feeding and food insecurity. Data convergence from multiple sources, referred to as triangulation, can strengthen the validity of the case study account.[10]

My multiple strategies and multiple sources of data allowed me to analyze all three intersections of social relations: social practice, social conditions, and the external relations that shape them. Furthermore, the contradictions I found highlight the need for policy developments to support infant food security.

Finding Formula

As an offshoot of the case study, I conducted further interviews with food bank and CPNP representatives beyond Nova Scotia. The rationale for this secondary study emerged from my initial interviews with women living in low-income circumstances as they talked about their efforts to find infant formula. The theme of infant food insecurity related to formula feeding, which is the focus of Chapter 4, was supported by data generated from asking program workers across Canada the following questions:

1. Can you tell me a bit about your organization's main goals, programs, and services?
2. Can you explain your and/or your organization's role in responding to the emergency food needs of families, and specifically of infants? Does this happen? Which family member typically approaches you?
3. What formal written policies concerning infant formula does your organization have, if any?
4. Now, what about informal policy? For example, do you follow any unwritten rules concerning formula?
5. Tell me what you do (or how your organization responds) to a family's emergency need for infant formula. What would happen if the need was constant? What challenges might there be in responding to this need?
6. What about other community organizations? Do you know where else those in need of infant formula might go? What do you think happens when they do so?
7. In general, how would you describe the nature of community need and community support for formula in low-income families? Could you explain any barriers to access?

Who? The Participants

The following are qualitative descriptions of the mothers I interviewed, detailing their demographic information and their infant feeding and food insecurity experiences. The names are pseudonyms.

Anne

Anne was twenty-two and lived alone with her twenty-month-old son in an apartment in a small town. She had completed high school and a community college program. At the time of the interview, she had no paid employment and her income was $1,061 per month from a combination of income assistance and child tax benefits. She had planned to breastfeed her son, yet after one week she switched to formula feeding. Anne had needed to use food banks, borrow money from family, and seek other food charity options since becoming a mother.

Mary

Mary was a thirty-three-year-old mother of seven who was pregnant at the time of the interview. Her fifteen-year-old child lived in foster care, her twelve-year-old lived with the child's father, and she lived alone with her other children, aged ten, nine, seven, three, and two. Mary lived in subsidized housing in a small town and had not completed high school. She had recently been employed full time, but prenatal health issues caused her to stop working and seek income assistance. Mary's monthly income comprised a combination of income assistance, child tax benefits, and a mere $9 in child support for one child, for a total $2,382. She had relied extensively on food charity to feed her family throughout her time as a mother.

Sally

Sally was twenty-three and lived in a small town with her fiancé and their eight-month-old daughter and her four- and two-year-old children from a previous relationship. She had completed Grade 12. Her household income came from her partner's full-time earnings and her child tax benefits, totalling $4,770 per month. When Sally lived on income assistance as a single parent, she ran out of food every month and routinely needed to borrow money and visit food banks.

Jean

Jean was twenty-four and lived with her boyfriend and her two sons, aged three years and nine months. Her three-year-old's twin had died soon after a premature birth. Her adult brother was also a household member. She lived in a rural town and had a Grade 9 education. Jean's household income came from her boyfriend's full-time earning and her child tax benefits, totalling approximately $3,000 per month. Her brother contributed to the household expenses as well. Jean had previously been on income assistance when she lived alone with her three-year-old. She grew up in a food insecure household and routinely experienced stress related to food insecurity as an adult. She stated that she thought she may be a food hoarder as a result. When she was living on income assistance she had needed to use food banks.

Heather

Heather was twenty-eight and lived with her partner and three children, aged seven, three, and fifteen months. She lived in an apartment in an urban area, had completed high school, and had attended community college. She had just begun providing in-home child care, and her partner worked at a job with fluctuating hours. They also received child tax benefits, and had an income of $2,000 per month on average. Heather was a frequent user of food banks and had received food charity from the Salvation Army and a family resource centre. She had also resorted to stealing food when necessary.

Cathy

Cathy was twenty-eight and lived alone with her four children, aged eleven, eight, two, and eight months. She lived in a small town and had completed high school. She usually worked part time but was on maternity leave at the time of the interview. Her income of $2,538 per month came from a combination of maternity benefits, child tax benefits, and child support payments. Cathy had lived on income assistance for several years when her first two children were younger. She had experienced household food insecurity throughout her time as a mother, seeking food from a variety of community charities and borrowing money from family and friends to secure food.

Margaret

Margaret was twenty-four and lived with her partner and their eight-month-old and her three children: seven-year-old twins and a five-year-old. She lived in a small town and had not completed high school. Her partner had a child from a previous relationship who did not live with them. Margaret's partner worked full time, and the monthly household income was approximately $3,000 combining earnings and child tax benefits. Margaret lived on income assistance prior to her current relationship. She had experienced household food insecurity particularly when she was a single parent living on income assistance. She still struggled with keeping enough food in the house but had never sought food charity.

Rosemary

Rosemary was twenty-three and lived with her partner and two children, one two years old and the other five weeks old. She had completed Grade 12 and lived rurally. Rosemary's partner worked full time. Their total monthly household income was approximately $4,000 from waged earnings and child tax benefits. Rosemary's experience of food insecurity was in relation to food quality and feeding issues.

Susan

Susan was twenty-four and lived alone with her three children, aged three, two, and four months. She had completed Grade 12 and lived in a rural town in low-income housing. Susan's monthly income of $2,397 comprised income assistance, child tax benefits, and child support payments. Although she was not currently using food banks, Susan had done so frequently in the past.

Beverly

Beverly was a twenty-nine-year-old woman who lived with her partner and three children, aged nine, seven, and six months. She had graduated from university and lived in an urban setting. Her partner worked full time and she received child tax benefits, for a total monthly household income of approximately $3,000. She had needed to use food banks sporadically over the years.

Kimberly

Kimberly was a twenty-nine-year-old woman who lived with her fiancé and three children, aged twelve, six, and twenty-three months. She had completed Grade 12 and lived in an urban area. Her husband worked full time and his earnings, combined with child tax benefits, totalled approximately $4,000 per month. Kimberly and her husband were burdened with debt, which affected their ability to cover basic needs. Prior to this relationship, she had received income assistance as a single parent in the province of Ontario, where she needed to use food banks and borrow money to secure food for her family. She did not use food banks at the time of the interview but had taken out payday loans for the last four years in order to keep food in the house.

Angela

Angela was twenty-nine and lived alone with her four children, aged nine, five, four, and eight months. She lived in an urban area and had less than a Grade 12 education. Her income consisted of income assistance and child tax benefits totalling $1,914 per month. Angela struggled constantly with household food insecurity. She had used food banks extensively, borrowed money, and stolen food when necessary.

Lorraine

Lorraine was twenty-four and lived in an urban setting with her husband and two children, aged three years and eight months. She had graduated from community college and was working three hours a week at the time of the interview. Her husband had been temporarily laid off from a full-time job and was awaiting employment insurance. Prior to the layoff, the monthly household income had totalled approximately $2,600 from a combination of earnings and child tax benefits. Lorraine and her partner had needed to borrow money for food. They had never gone to a food bank, but Lorraine indicated that she was seeking information on food banks in her area.

Elaine

Elaine was twenty-seven and lived alone with her two children, aged three years and four months, in a low-income housing complex in an urban setting. She had a Grade 12 education. She received income assistance and child tax benefits for a monthly income of $1,100 excluding rent and power, which were paid to the housing complex directly by the provincial income assistance program. Elaine was a frequent user of food banks and other food charity options as she lived in a constant state of food insecurity.

Erica

Erica was twenty-nine and lived in an urban area with her husband and three children: a four-year-old, a two-year-old, and a baby of three months. Erica had completed Grade 12 and a community college program. She was on maternity leave from her full-time job as a hair stylist at the time of the interview. Her husband worked full time and she considered her family to be fortunate, but due to their reduced income during maternity leave money was tight. Her monthly income was approximately $3,500. Erica had never sought food charity.

Jessica

Jessica was twenty and lived in an urban apartment with an elderly roommate and her baby, who was ten months old. Jessica had not completed high school. Her rent was paid directly by the provincial income assistance program, and she received an additional $255 from income assistance, plus $323 in child tax benefits monthly, totalling $578. Jessica had a history of food insecurity, particularly when she was pregnant and living in a shelter. She still struggled not to run out of food each month and had to use food charity sources and borrow money to buy formula. She had also used pawn shops in order to secure small amounts of money to buy food and diapers, but stated that she had nothing left to pawn. She had also used a payday loan service, which she had not been able to repay.

Emily

Emily was thirty and lived with her partner and their twelve-month-old child, who had recently been returned to them after living in foster care as a result of a child protection order in place since the child's birth. Emily had not completed high school. She had four children from a previous relationship – aged thirteen, twelve, ten, and five – for whom she had joint custody. They lived primarily with their father, a four-hour drive away. Her household income of $1,600 per month consisted of income assistance disability payments to her partner (following a car accident) and child tax benefits. Emily had used food banks and other food charity options over the years.

Sarah

Sarah was twenty-five and lived in an urban area with her two children, aged twenty-two months and four months. She had completed her Grade 12 equivalency. Her income was a combination of income assistance and child tax benefits totalling $1,706 per month. Sarah struggled regularly with food insecurity and had used food banks and other food charity options.

Emma

Emma was forty-two and lived with her four children in a low-income housing complex in a rural town. She had completed high school along with some university-level education. Her children were twelve, eight, two, and two months old. Emma had recently separated from her husband and had needed to secure income assistance since living apart from him. Her combined monthly income from income assistance and child tax benefits was $1,488. Emma was experiencing food insecurity at the time of the interview and was using the local food bank.

Hannah

Hannah was twenty-seven and lived in a house in a small town with her partner and three children, aged six, three, and three months. Hannah had a Grade 10 education. Her partner worked full time at a fast-food restaurant. Their income of $2,300 month was a combination of his earnings and child tax benefits. Hannah had experienced household food insecurity throughout her parenthood and needed to use food banks. She had in the past resorted to stealing food when necessary.

Socio-demographic Summary

Table 1 summarizes the socio-demographic characteristics of the mothers who were interviewed. As can be seen, the women were relatively young; only two were over thirty and the rest were between the ages of twenty and thirty. Seventeen of the twenty self-identified as white Canadians, one self-identified as mixed race, and two self-identified as Aboriginal. Three white mothers described one or more of their children as mixed race. Half the women lived in urban areas and half rurally.

The average family size was 5 people, ranging from two (a mother and one child) to six (two parents and four children or one parent and five children). Two mothers had only one child, five had two children, and thirteen had more than three. The fertility rate of the group – the average number of children per woman – was 3, which is twice the rate for Nova Scotian women as a whole, calculated at 1.50 for the year 2009.[11] The twenty mothers interviewed had a total of sixty-one children, ranging in age from five weeks to fifteen years.

Not all the children resided within the household on a full-time basis. In one case, three of the interviewee's four children split their time between her home and their father's. One mother of seven had a child who resided in permanent foster care and another who lived with the child's father. Eight women were single parents living alone with their children, eleven lived with their children and a partner, and one lived with her child and a roommate.

It is important to note that while all the women had at least one child between six and twenty-four months and were asked to describe their feeding experiences within the first year of their youngest child's life, they talked about feeding all their children during infancy and beyond. It was important to consider their diverse feeding histories. Some of the women moved in and out of food insecure conditions, making it possible to reflect on how changes in their life circumstances shaped the way they fed all their babies.

The interviewees had lower educational attainment than the average Nova Scotian. For example, they were more likely not to have completed Grade 12 (35 percent, compared to the provincial rate of 31.7 percent) and less likely to have education beyond high school (30 percent, compared to 51.8 percent).[12] Only 15 percent were working in any capacity outside the home at the time of being interviewed.

The median income of the group ($2,390 per month, or $28,680 annually) was less than half the median total income of families in the province ($5,502 per month, or $66,030 annually) in 2011.[13] Household income in

TABLE 1
Socio-demographic characteristics of interviewed mothers

Characteristic	Category	Number of mothers (N = 20)
Age	20–25	9
	26–30	9
	31–35	1
	36–40	–
	41–45	1
Ethnicity (self-described)	White	17
	Aboriginal	2
	Mixed	1
Education	< Grade 12	7
	Grade 12	7
	Community college	4
	Some university	1
	Completed university	1
Other household members	Child/ren	8
	Partner and child/ren	11
	Roommate and child/ren	1
Number of children	1	2
	2	5
	3+	13
Location of home	Rural	10
	Urban	10
Employment status	Working full time	–
	Working part time	1
	On maternity leave	2
	Not working	17
Monthly income	<$1000	1
	$1,001–2,000	7
	$2,001–3,000	8
	>$3,000	4

each instance depended on the number of children and adults, as well as the type of income sources each family had access to. The interviewees identified five distinct income sources: employment earnings, child tax benefits (the Canada Child Tax Benefit and the Universal Child Care Benefit),[14] provincial income assistance (general income assistance and disability income assistance), federal maternity leave benefits, and child support payments. All households received the Child Tax Benefit and the Universal Child Care Benefit. Nine mothers received provincial income assistance at the time of the interviews, and seventeen had been on income assistance at one time or another since becoming mothers. Although eight were single parents (all of them on income assistance except for one case of maternity leave), only three received any child support as a component of their total income. Of these three, one received federal maternity benefits that were unaffected by the receipt of child support. The other two had their child support payments deducted dollar for dollar from their income assistance entitlement.

Notes

Introduction: The Invisibility of Infant Food Insecurity

1 S.A. Anderson, "Core Indicators of Nutritional State for Difficult-to-Sample Populations," *Journal of Nutrition* 120 (1990): 1559–600.

2 J. Chen and J. Che, "Food Insecurity in Canadian Households," *Health Reports* 12, 4 (2001): 11–22; Nicholas T. Vozoris and Valerie S. Tarasuk, "Household Food Insufficiency Is Associated with Poorer Health," *Journal of Nutrition* 133, 1 (2003): 120–26.

3 Kathy L. Radimer et al., "Understanding Hunger and Developing Indicators to Assess It in Women and Children," *Journal of Nutrition Education* 24, 1, supplement 1 (1992): 36S–45S.

4 Valerie Tarasuk, Andy Mitchell, and Naomi Dachner, *Household Food Insecurity in Canada, 2014* (Toronto: Research to Identify Policy Options to Reduce Food Insecurity [PROOF], 2016), https://proof.utoronto.ca.

5 For Nova Scotia, see Voices for Food Security in Nova Scotia, *Can Nova Scotians Afford to Eat Healthy? Report on 2015 Participatory Food Costing*, (Halifax: Food Action Research Centre [FoodARC], Mount Saint Vincent University, 2017), https://foodarc.ca. For other Canadian provinces, see *Food Costing in BC 2017* (Vancouver: BC Centre for Disease Control, 2018); Nicholas Vozoris, Barbara Davis, and Valerie Tarasuk, "The Affordability of a Nutritious Diet for Households on Welfare in Toronto," *Canadian Journal of Public Health* 93, 1 (2002): 36–40.

6 Karen Rideout, Barbara Seed, and Aleck Ostry, "Putting Food on the Public Health Table: Making Food Security Relevant to Regional Health Authorities," *Canadian Journal of Public Health* 97, 3 (2006): 233–36.

7 Lynn McIntyre and Laura Anderson, "Food Insecurity," in *Social Determinants of Health: Canadian Perspectives*, ed. Dennis Raphael, 294–320 (Toronto: Canadian

Scholars' Press, 2016); Valerie Tarasuk, "Health Implications of Food Insecurity," in *Social Determinants of Health*, ed. Raphael, 321–42.

8 Reynaldo Martorell, "Improved Nutrition in the First 1000 Days and Adult Human Capital and Health," *American Journal of Human Biology* 29, 2 (2017): e22952, https://doi.org/10.1002/ajhb.22952; D.J.P. Barker, "The Developmental Origins of Adult Disease," *Journal of the American College of Nutrition* 23, supplement 6 (2004): 588S–95S.

9 Sharon I. Kirkpatrick, Lynn McIntyre, and Melissa L. Potestio, "Child Hunger and Long-Term Adverse Consequences for Health," *Archives of Pediatrics and Adolescent Medicine* 164, 8 (2010): 754–62; Lynn McIntyre et al., "Depression and Suicide Ideation in Late Adolescence and Early Adulthood Are an Outcome of Child Hunger," *Journal of Affective Disorders* 150, 1 (2013): 123–29. Research from the United States also clearly links household food insecurity to negative health outcomes for infants: Ann E. Bryant Borders et al., "Chronic Stress and Low Birth Weight Neonates in a Low-Income Population of Women," *Obstetrics and Gynecology* 109, 2, part 1 (2007): 331–38; John T. Cook et al., "Food Insecurity Is Associated with Adverse Health Outcomes among Human Infants and Toddlers," *Journal of Nutrition* 134, 6 (2004): 1432–38; Katherine Alaimo et al., "Food Insufficiency, Family Income, and Health in US Preschool and School-Aged Children," *American Journal of Public Health* 91, 5 (2001): 781–86; Ruth Rose-Jacobs et al., "Household Food Insecurity: Associations with At-Risk Infant and Toddler Development," *Pediatrics* 121, 1 (2008): 65–72; Hernandez and Jacknowitz, 2009; Anne Skalicky et al., "Child Food Insecurity and Iron Deficiency Anemia in Low-Income Infants and Toddlers in the United States," *Maternal and Child Health Journal* 10, 2 (2006): 177–85; Kyong Park et al., "Household Food Insecurity Is a Risk Factor for Iron-Deficiency Anaemia in a Multi-ethnic, Low-Income Sample of Infants and Toddlers," *Public Health Nutrition* 12, 11 (2009): 2120–28; Martha Zaslow et al., "Food Security during Infancy: Implications for Attachment and Mental Proficiency in Toddlerhood," *Maternal and Child Health Journal* 13, 1 (2009): 66–80.

10 Kate Bezanson, "The Neo-Liberal State and Social Reproduction: Gender and Household Insecurity in the Late 1990s," in *Social Reproduction: Feminist Political Economy Challenges Neo-Liberalism*, ed. Kate Bezanson and Meg Luxton (Montreal and Kingston: McGill-Queen's University Press, 2006), 175.

11 Marjorie L. DeVault, *Feeding the Family: The Social Organization of Caring as Gendered Work* (Chicago: University of Chicago Press, 1991); Nickie Charles and Marion Kerr, "Food for Feminist Thought," *Sociological Review* 34, 3 (1986): 537–72; Brenda Beagan et al., "'It's Just Easier for Me to Do It': Rationalizing the Family Division of Foodwork," *Sociology* 42, 4 (2008): 653–71; Kate Cairns and Josée Johnson, *Food and Femininity* (New York: Bloomsbury, 2015).

12 Susan Braedley, "Someone to Watch over You: Gender, Class, and Social Reproduction," in *Social Reproduction,* ed. Bezanson and Luxton, 216.

13 Monica Townson and Kevin Hayes, *Women and the Employment Insurance Program* (Toronto: Canadian Centre for Policy Alternatives, 2007), http://www.policyalter natives.ca.

14 The Family Supplement to Maternity Benefits is in place to improve the incomes of low-income families, but the eligibility threshold has not increased since its implementation in 1998, and it sits thousands of dollars below Statistics Canada's 2017 low income measure after-tax thresholds for a single parent with one child ($30,029), a couple with one child ($36,778), or a couple with two children ($42,468). Only 44 percent of families outside Quebec with annual incomes lower than $30,000 receive employment insurance maternity/parental benefits at all, because they either are not eligible or they do not apply. See Lindsey McKay, Sophie Mathieu, and Andrea Doucet, "Parental-Leave Rich and Parental-Leave Poor: Inequality in Canadian Labour Market Based Leave Policies," *Journal of Industrial Relations* 58, 4 (2016): 543–62.

15 "Gender Wage Gap (indicator)," OECD, latest data available accessed November 14, 2019, https://data.oecd.org/earnwage/gender-wage-gap.htm.

16 Patricia Evans, "Eroding Canadian Social Welfare: The Mulroney Legacy, 1984–1993," in *Social Fabric or Patchwork Quilt: The Development of Social Policy in Canada,* ed. Raymond B. Black and Jeffrey A. Keshen (Toronto, Broadview Press, 2006), 263–74.

17 "Fact Sheet: Woman and Poverty in Canada," Canadian Women's Foundation, February 2017, https://www.canadianwomen.org/wp-content/uploads/2017/09/Facts-About-Women-and-Poverty.pdf; Statistics Canada, *Census in Brief: Children Living in Low-Income Households* Catalogue no. 98-200-X2016012 (Ottawa: Statistics Canada, 2017), http://www12.statcan.gc.ca/census-recensement/2016/as-sa/98-200-x/2016012/98-200-x2016012-eng.cfm.

18 Vanessa Maher, *The Anthropology of Breast-Feeding: Natural Law or Social Construct* (Providence, RI: Berg Publishers, 1992); Paige Hall Smith, Bernice L. Hausman, and Miriam Labbok, eds., Beyond Health, *Beyond Choice: Breastfeeding Constraints and Realities* (New Brunswick, NJ: Rutgers University Press, 2012).

19 Lora Ebert Wallace and Holly Chason, "Infant Feeding in the Modern World: Medicalization and the Maternal Body," *Sociological Spectrum* 27, 4 (2007): 405–38.

20 "Trends in Breastfeeding Practices in Canada (2001 to 2009–2010)," Health Canada, last modified April 24, 2012, http://www.hc-sc.gc.ca/fn-an/surveill/nutrition/commun/prenatal/trends-tendances-eng.php

21 Gabrielle Palmer, *The Politics of Breastfeeding: When Breasts Are Bad for Business* (London: Pandora Press, 2009), 12.

22 Valerie Fildes, "The Culture and Biology of Breastfeeding: An Historical Review of Western Europe," in *Breastfeeding: Biocultural Perspectives,* ed. Patricia Stuart-Macadam and Katherine A. Dettwyler (New York: Aldine De Gruyter, 1995), 101.

23 Tarasuk, Mitchell, and Dachner, *Household Food Insecurity in Canada, 2014.*

24 Healthy Eating Action Group of the Nova Scotia Alliance for Healthy Eating and Physical Activity, *Healthy Eating Nova Scotia,* policy document produced in partnership with the Office of Health Promotion, March 2005, https://novascotia.ca/dhw/healthy-communities/documents/Provincial-Healthy-Eating-Strategy.pdf.

25 Farryl M.W. Bertmann and Amy L. Yaroch, "Role of Breast Milk and Breastfeeding within the Context of a Sustainable, Resilient Food System," *Journal of Hunger and Environmental Nutrition* 11, 2 (2016): 242–53; Cathleen Kneen, "Breastfeeding: A Paradigm of a Sustainable Food System," unpublished PDF, 2008, https://foodsecurecanada.org/sites/foodsecurecanada.org/files/Breastfeeding.pdf; Susan B. Draper, "Breast-Feeding as a Sustainable Resource System," A*merican Anthropologist* 98, 2 (1996): 258–65; Libby Salmon, "Food Security for Infants and Young Children: An Opportunity for Breastfeeding Policy?" *International Breastfeeding Journal* 10, 7 (2015): n.p., https://doi.org/10.1186/s13006-015-0029-6; Infact Canada, *Breastfeeding and Food Security: The High Cost of Formula Feeding,* (Rockport, ON: Infact Canada, 2004), http://www.infactcanada.ca/Breastfeeding_and_Food_Security.pdf; Ruth A. Lawrence, "The Eradication of Poverty One Child at a Time through Breastfeeding: A Contribution to the Global Theme Issue on Poverty and Human Development," *Breastfeeding Medicine* 2, 4 (2007): 193–94.

26 S.L. Huffman et al., *Breastfeeding: A Natural Resource for Food Security,* USAID Cooperative Agreement no. DPE-5966-A-00-1045-00 (Washington, DC: Wellstart International, 1992), 27.

27 On high rates of infant mortality and morbidity in the developing world, see Penny Van Esterik, *Beyond the Breast-Bottle Controversy* (New Brunswick, NJ: Rutgers University Press, 1989); D.B. Jelliffe and E.F.P. Jelliffe, *Human Milk in the Modern World* (Oxford: Oxford University Press, 1978); Palmer, *The Politics of Breastfeeding*; on Canadian populations, see Tasnim Nathoo and Aleck Ostry, *The One Best Way? Breastfeeding History, Politics, and Policy in Canada* (Waterloo, ON: Wilfred Laurier University Press, 2009), 118.

28 On formula affordability, see Infact Canada, "The Cost of Formula and Infant Feeding Security," *INFACT Canada Newsletter* (Fall 1997): n.p., http://www.infactcanada.ca/security.htm. On formula contamination and preparation issues, see Erica Weir, "Powdered Infant Formula and Fatal Infection with *Enterobacter sakazakii*," *Canadian Medical Association Journal* 166, 12 (2002): 1570; Food and Agriculture Organization and the World Health Organization (FAO and WHO), Enterobacter Sakazakii *and Other Microorganisms in Powdered Infant Formula,* Microbiological Risk Assessment

Series no. 6, meeting report (Geneva: FAO/WHO, 2004); Ted Greiner, "Beyond Melamine: More Reasons Not to Use Animal Milk in Infant Feeding," *Journal of Human Lactation* 25, 4 (2009): 397–99; R. Lakshman, D. Ogilvie, and K.K. Ong, "Mothers' Experiences of Bottle-Feeding: A Systematic Review of Qualitative and Quantitative Studies," *Archives of Disease in Childhood* 94, 8 (2009): 596–601; Salmon, "Food Security for Infants and Young Children." On the environmental costs linked to bottle feeding, see Palmer, *The Politics of Breastfeeding*; A. Radford, *The Ecological Impact of Bottle Feeding*, Report for Baby Milk Action (Cambridge: IBFAN, 1991). On the cost to the health care system, see Thomas M. Ball and Anne L. Wright, "Health Care Costs of Formula-Feeding in the First Year of Life," *Pediatrics* 103, 4, part 2 (1999): 870–76. On supply shortages due to increased global demand and unregulated trade, see Salmon, "Food Security for Infants and Young Children."

29 Food and Agriculture Organization (FAO), Rome Declaration on World Food Security and World Food Summit Plan of Action (Rome: FAO, 1996).

30 Canada, Department of Agriculture and Agri-Food, *Canada's Action Plan for Food Security*, report produced in response to the World Food Summit Plan for Action, 1998, http://www.agr.gc.ca/misb/fsec-seca/pdf/action_e.pdf.

31 Catherine L. Mah et al., "A Frame-Critical Policy Analysis of Canada's Response to World Food Summit 1998–2008," *Archives of Public Health* 72, 41 (2014): 1–7. See also Laura Payton, "UN Official Sparks Debate over Canadian Food Security," *CBC News*, May 16, 2012, http://www.cbc.ca/news/politics/un-official-sparks-debate-over-canadian-food-security-1.1130281.

32 "A Food Policy for Canada," Government of Canada, last modified August 12, 2019, https://www.canada.ca/en/agriculture-agri-food/news/2019/08/everyone-at-the-table-minister-bibeau-highlights-investments-to-improve-access-to-local-food-as-part-of-the-food-policy-for-canada.html.

33 Graham Riches, *Food Bank Nations: Poverty, Corporate Charity and the Right to Food* (New York: Routledge, 2018).

34 Public Health Agency of Canada, *The Canada Prenatal Nutrition Program: A Decade of Promoting the Health of Mothers, Babies and Communities* (Ottawa: Minister of Health, 2007).

Chapter 1: Doing Without

1 Patricia Evans, "Eroding Canadian Social Welfare: The Mulroney Legacy, 1984–1993," in *Social Fabric or Patchwork Quilt: The Development of Social Policy in Canada*, ed. Raymond B. Black and Jeffrey A. Keshen (Toronto, Broadview Press, 2006), 266.

2 "Nova Scotia Child Benefit," Government of Nova Scotia, last modified July 4, 2012, https://novascotia.ca/coms/families/ChildBenefit.html.

3 At the time of the interviews, child support was clawed back from income assistance recipients in Nova Scotia. According to the federal Department of Justice website on

child support, "Children need financial support from their parents – and they have a legal right to it" ("Child Support," Department of Justice, last modified August 8, 2017, http://justice.gc.ca/eng/fl-df/child-enfant/index.html), yet the treatment of child support/maintenance payments for those on social/income assistance varies regionally. British Columbia, the Northwest Territories, and Ontario exempt child support payments from calculations of income support. As of August 2018, the Nova Scotia Department of Community Services justly stopped deducting child support payments from income assistant recipients.

4 Cathy's case presents another picture. Her income consisted of maternity benefits, child support, and child benefits, and she considered herself to be better off financially on maternity leave than when she was on income assistance. This was partly because child support had been deducted from her income assistance entitlements, but while she was on maternity leave her child-maintenance payments did not affect her benefits and she therefore considered it helpful. Child support did need to be declared as "other monies," but because it was not considered earnings for the purpose of employment, it was not clawed back.

5 Peter Andrée et al., "Structural Constraints and Enablers to Community Food Security in Nova Scotia, Canada," *Journal of Hunger and Environmental Nutrition* 11, 4 (2016): 456–90; Patricia L. Williams et al., "Affordability of a Nutritious Diet for Income Assistance Recipients in Nova Scotia (2002–2010)," *Canadian Journal of Public Health* 103, 3 (2012): 183–88; Kim D. Travers, "The Social Organization of Nutritional Inequities," *Social Science and Medicine* 43, 4 (1996): 543–53; Valerie Tarasuk, *Household and Individual Food Insecurity,* discussion paper prepared for the Office of Nutrition Policy and Promotion (Ottawa: Health Canada, 2001); Cathy C. Campbell and Ellen Desjardins, "A Model and Research Approach for Studying the Management of Limited Food Resources by Low Income Families," *Journal of Nutrition Education and Behavior* 21, 4 (1989): 162–71; Elaine M. Power, "Determinants of Healthy Eating among Low-Income Canadians," *Canadian Journal of Public Health* 96, 3 (2005): S37–42.

6 Maureen Baker, "Child Poverty, Maternal Health and Social Benefits," *Current Sociology* 50, 6 (2002): 823–83; Travers, "The Social Organization of Nutritional Inequities"; Sharon I. Kirkpatrick and Valerie Tarasuk, "Adequacy of Food Spending Is Related to Housing Expenditures among Lower-Income Canadian Households," *Public Health Nutrition* 10, 12 (2007): 1464–73; John Mirowsky and Catherine E. Ross. "Economic Hardship across the Life Course," *American Sociological Review* 64, 4 (1999): 548–69.

7 Kathy L. Radimer et al., "Understanding Hunger and Developing Indicators to Assess It in Women and Children," *Journal of Nutrition Education* 24, 1, supplement 1 (1992): 36S–45S.

8 Pierre Bourdieu, *Distinction: A Social Critique of the Judgement of Taste,* trans. Richard Nice (Cambridge, MA: Harvard University Press, 1984).

9 *Canada's Food Guide* is a nutrition education tool produced by Health Canada to help people follow a healthy diet. See https://food-guide.canada.ca/en/.

10 The father of Anne's child was a migrant farm worker, and Anne spoke about how vegetable and fruit consumption in her household was much improved in the summer months when he was in the country, as he could bring produce from the farm he worked on.

11 Felicia D. Newell, Patricia L. Williams, and Cynthia G. Watt, "Is the Minimum Enough? Affordability of a Nutritious Diet for Minimum Wage Earners in Nova Scotia (2002–2012)," *Canadian Journal of Public Health* 105, 3 (2014): e158–65; Williams et al., "Affordability of a Nutritious Diet"; Patricia L. Williams et al., "Can Households Earning Minimum Wage in Nova Scotia Afford a Nutritious Diet?" *Canadian Journal of Public Health* 97, 6 (2006): 430–34.

12 Lynn McIntyre et al., "Do Low-Income Lone Mothers Compromise Their Nutrition to Feed Their Children?" *Canadian Medical Association Journal* 168 (2003): 686–91.

13 Brendine Partyka et al., "Infant Nutrition in Saskatoon: Barriers to Infant Food Security," *Canadian Journal of Dietetic Practice and Research* 71, 2 (2010): 79–84; Anne-Marie Hamelin, Micheline Beaudry, and Jean-Pierre Habicht, "Characterization of Household Food Insecurity in Québec: Food and Feelings," *Social Science and Medicine* 54, 1 (2002): 119–32; James D. Ford and Maude Beaumier, "Feeding the Family during Times of Stress: Experience and Determinants of Food Insecurity in an Inuit Community," *Geographical Journal* 177, 1 (2011): 44–61; Maude C. Beaumier and James D. Ford, "Food Insecurity among Inuit Women Exacerbated by Socio-economic Stresses and Climate Change," *Canadian Journal of Public Health* 101, 3 (2010): 196–201; Valerie Tarasuk and Heather Maclean, "The Food Problems of Low-Income Single Mothers: An Ethnographic Study," *Canadian Home Economics Journal* 40, 2 (1990): 76–82; Radimer et al., "Understanding Hunger and Developing Indicators"; Travers, "The Social Organization of Nutritional Inequities."

14 It would be presumptuous to claim that children in these families would eat with their parents if food deprivation were not a condition, or that parents and children eat together in other families for that matter. As Anne Murcott argues, there is little evidence to suggest that doing so is a family food norm, even though the idea that the family meal is in decline is readily used as an indication of societal decline ("Family Meals – A Thing of the Past?" in *Food, Health and Identity,* ed. Pat Caplan [New York: Routledge, 1997], 32–50).

15 Marjorie L. DeVault, *Feeding the Family: The Social Organization of Caring as Gendered Work* (Chicago: University of Chicago Press, 1991).

16 Carole M. Counihan, *Around the Tuscan Table: Food, Family, and Gender in Twentieth-Century Florence* (New York: Routledge, 2004); Alice P. Julier, *Eating Together: Food, Friendship, and Inequality* (Urbana: University of Illinois Press, 2013).

17 Sheila Mammen, Jean W. Bauer, and Leslie Richards, "Understanding Persistent Food Insecurity: A Paradox of Place and Circumstance," *Social Indicators Research* 92 (2009): 151–68; Janet Poppendieck, *Sweet Charity? Emergency Food and the End of Entitlement* (New York: Penguin, 1998); Valerie S. Tarasuk and George H. Beaton, "Household Food Insecurity and Hunger among Families Using Food Banks," *Canadian Journal of Public Health* 90, 2 (1999): 109–13; Karen Hobbs et al., "Waste of a Nation: Poor People Speak Out about Charity," *Canadian Review of Social Policy* 31 (1993): 94–104; Linda Jacobs-Starkey, Harriet V. Kuhnlein, and Katherine Gray-Donald, "Food Bank Users: Sociodemographic and Nutritional Characteristics," *Canadian Medical Association Journal* 158, 9 (1998): 1143–49.

18 Graham Riches, "Hunger, Food Security and Welfare Policies: Issues and Debates in First World Societies," *Proceedings of the Nutrition Society* 56 (1997): 62–74; Graham Riches, *Food Bank Nations: Poverty, Corporate Charity and the Right to Food* (New York: Routledge, 2018); Tarasuk and Maclean, "The Food Problems of Low-Income Singe Mothers"; Valerie Tarasuk and Barbara Davis, "Responses to Food Insecurity in the Changing Canadian Welfare State," *Journal of Nutrition Education* 28, 2 (1996): 71–75.

19 Tarasuk, Household and Individual Food Insecurity.

20 Riches, *Food Bank Nations*; Barbara Davis and Valerie Tarasuk, "Hunger in Canada," *Agriculture and Human Values* 11, 4 (1994): 50–57; Poppendieck, *Sweet Charity?*; Power, ; Valerie Tarasuk and Joan M. Eakin, "Charitable Food Assistance as Symbolic Gesture: An Ethnographic Study of Food Banks in Ontario," *Social Science and Medicine* 56, 7 (2003): 1505–15.

21 Graham Riches, "Food Banks and Food Security: Welfare Reform, Human Rights and Social Policy," *Social Policy and Administration* 36, 6 (2002): 648–63.

22 Counihan, *Around the Tuscan Table*; Nickie Charles and Marion Kerr, *Women, Food, and Families* (Manchester: Manchester University Press, 1988); DeVault, *Feeding the Family*.

23 Hannah also referred to routinely cutting large roasts of meat in half as a strategy for stretching the household food supply.

24 Carol M. Devine et al., "Sandwiching It In: Spillover of Work onto Food Choices and Family Roles in Low- and Moderate-Income Urban Households," *Social Science and Medicine* 56, 3 (2003): 617–30.

25 A purchase order is a food voucher that individuals on income assistance sometimes get access to. If a food order is provided, the amount of the order will be deducted from their next monthly income assistance cheque. This is usually not a preferred option for getting food, as it tends to make securing food the next month even harder; however, it is sometimes necessary when the food bank will be closed for several days or if the person has already been to the food bank recently and is temporarily ineligible.

26 Child protection matters in Nova Scotia are the domain of the Department of Community Services, carried out under the Child and Family Services Act.

27 Radimer et al., "Understanding Hunger and Developing Indicators."

28 A condensed presentation of this typology appears in Lesley Frank, "Exploring Infant Feeding Practices in Food Insecure Households: What Is the Real Issue?" *Food and Foodways: Explorations in the History and Culture of Human Nourishment* 23, 3 (2015): 186–209. Reprinted by permission of the publisher (Taylor & Francis Ltd, http://www.tandfonline.com).

Chapter 2: When Breastfeeding Works

1 This review of the framing of public policy related to infant food insecurity in Canada first appeared in Lesley Frank, "The Breastfeeding Paradox: A Critique of Policy Related to Infant Food Insecurity in Canada," *Food, Culture and Society* 8, 1 (2015): 107–29. © The Association for the Study of Food & Society (ASFS), reprinted by permission of Taylor & Francis Ltd, www.tandfonline.com.

2 United Nations Office of the High Commissioner for Human Rights, *Universal Declaration of Human Rights*, adopted by General Assembly Resolution 217A, December 10, 1948, https://undocs.org/A/RES/217(III).

3 United Nations Office of the High Commissioner for Human Rights, *International Covenant on Economic, Social and Cultural Rights*, adopted by General Assembly Resolution 2200A (XXI), December 16, 1966, https://www.ohchr.org/en/professional interest/pages/cescr.aspx.

4 United Nations Office of the High Commissioner for Human Rights, *CESCR General Comment No. 12: The Right to Adequate Food (Art. 11)*, adopted at the 20th session of the Committee on Economic, Social and Cultural Rights, May 12, 1999. https://www.refworld.org/pdfid/4538838c11.pdf.

5 Food and Agriculture Organization (FAO), Rome Declaration on World Food Security and World Food Summit Plan of Action (Rome: FAO, 1996).

6 United Nations Office of the High Commissioner for Human Rights, *Convention on the Rights of the Child*, adopted by General Assembly Resolution 44/25, November 20, 1989, https://www.ohchr.org/en/professionalinterest/pages/crc.aspx.

7 World Health Organization (WHO), *International Code of Marketing of Breast-Milk Substitutes* (Geneva: WHO, 1981), http://www.who.int/nutrition/publications/code_english.pdf; United Nations Children's Fund (UNICEF), *Innocenti Declaration: On the Protection, Promotion and Support of Breastfeeding*, WHO/UNICEF Policymakers' Meeting, Florence, July 30–August 1, 1990, http://www.unicef.org/programme/breastfeeding/innocenti.htm; UNICEF, *Innocenti Declaration 2005: On Infant and Young Child Feeding*, adopted at "Celebrating Innocenti 1990–2005:

Achievements, Challenges and Future Imperatives," November 22, 2005, http://innocenti15.net/declaration.pdf.pdf; "Baby-Friendly Hospital Initiative," WHO, accessed November 20, 2019, https://www.who.int/nutrition/topics/bfhi/en.

8 Abigail Friendly, *Towards Food Security Policy for Canada's Social Housing Sector*, Canadian Policy Research Networks Research Report (Ottawa: Canadian Social Policy Research Networks and Social Housing Services Corporation, 2008); Riches, 2002.

9 Canada, Department of Agriculture and Agri-Food, *Canada's Action Plan for Food Security,* report produced in response to the World Food Summit Plan for Action, 1998, http://www.agr.gc.ca/misb/fsec-seca/pdf/action_e.pdf.

10 Ibid., p. 6.

11 Health Canada, *Exclusive Breastfeeding Duration: 2004 Health Canada Recommendation,* Publication no. 4824 (Ottawa: Health Canada, 2004), http://publications.gc.ca/collections/Collection/H44-73-2004E.pdf.

12 Breastfeeding Committee of Canada, 2002.

13 Ibid.

14 Infact Canada, *Breastfeeding and Food Security: The High Cost of Formula Feeding* (Rockport, ON: Infact Canada, 2004), 1, http://www.infactcanada.ca/Breastfeeding_and_Food_Security.pdf. See also Infact Canada, "The Cost of Formula and Infant Feeding Security," *INFACT Canada Newsletter* (Fall 1997): n.p., http://www.infactcanada.ca/security.htm.

15 Cathleen Kneen, "Breastfeeding: A Paradigm of a Sustainable Food System," unpublished PDF, 2008, https://foodsecurecanada.org/sites/foodsecurecanada.org/files/Breastfeeding.pdf.

16 People's Food Policy Project, *Resetting the Table: A People's Food Policy for Canada* (Montreal: Food Secure Canada, 2011), 21, https://foodsecurecanada.org/sites/foodsecurecanada.org/files/FSC-resetting2012-8half11-lowres-EN.pdf.

17 Healthy Eating Action Group of the Nova Scotia Alliance for Healthy Eating and Physical Activity, *Healthy Eating Nova Scotia,* policy document produced in partnership with the Office of Health Promotion, March 2005, https://novascotia.ca/dhw/healthy-communities/documents/Provincial-Healthy-Eating-Strategy.pdf.; Ontario Food and Nutrition Strategy Group, *Ontario Food and Nutrition Strategy: A Comprehensive Evidence informed Plan for Healthy Food and Food Systems in Ontario,* policy document produced by Ontario Food and Nutrition Strategy Group, 2017.

18 Ruth A. Lawrence, "The Eradication of Poverty One Child at a Time through Breastfeeding: A Contribution to the Global Theme Issue on Poverty and Human Development," *Breastfeeding Medicine* 2, 4 (2007): 194.

Chapter 3: When Breastfeeding Fails

1 "Trends in Breastfeeding Practices in Canada (2001 to 2009–2010)," Health Canada, last modified April 24, 2012, http://www.hc-sc.gc.ca/fn-an/surveill/nutrition/commun/prenatal/trends-tendances-eng.php.

2 Five of the eight single mothers were primarily non-breastfeeders compared to three of the twelve women in two-parent families.

3 See Nancy F. Butte, Mardia G. López-Alarcón, and Cutberto Garza, *Nutrient Adequacy of Exclusive Breastfeeding for the Term Infant during the First Six Months of Life* (Geneva: World Health Organization, 2002), compared to L. Allen, "Maternal Micronutrient Malnutrition: Effects on Breast Milk and Infant Nutrition, and Priorities for Intervention," *SCN News* 11 (1994): 21–24; Gabrielle Palmer, *The Politics of Breastfeeding: When Breasts Are Bad for Business* (London: Pandora Press, 2009).

4 Kathryn Dewey, "Energy and Protein Requirements during Lactation," *Annual Review of Nutrition* 17 (1997): 19–36.

5 Michelle Kominiarek and Priya Rajan, "Nutrition Recommendations in Pregnancy and Lactation," *Medical Clinics of North America* 100, 6 (2016): 1199–215; Kelly Bonyata, "Do Breastfeeding Mothers Need Extra Calories or Fluids?" *KellyMom*, last modified March 10, 2019, http://kellymom.com/nutrition/mothers-diet/mom-calories-fluids.

6 L. Ricciuto, V. Tarasuk, and A. Yatchew, "Socio-Demographic Influences on Food Purchasing among Canadian Households," *European Journal of Clinical Nutrition* 60, 6 (2006): 778–90; Laurie Ricciuto and Valerie S. Tarasuk, "An Examination of Income-Related Disparities in the Nutritional Quality of Food Selections among Canadian Households from 1986–2001," *Social Science and Medicine* 64, 1 (2007): 186–98.

7 Voices for Food Security in Nova Scotia, *Can Nova Scotians Afford to Eat Healthy? Report on 2015 Participatory Food Costing* (Halifax: Food Action Research Centre [FoodARC], Mount Saint Vincent University, 2017), https://foodarc.ca.

8 Bernice L. Hausman, *Mother's Milk: Breastfeeding Controversies in American Culture* (New York: Routledge, 2003); Jacqueline C. Kent, Danielle K. Prime, and Catherine P. Garbin, "Principles for Maintaining or Increasing Breast Milk Production," *Journal of Obstetric, Gynecologic, and Neonatal Nursing* 41, 1 (2012): 114–21.

9 Claire Elizabeth Willis and Verity Livingstone, "Infant Insufficient Milk Syndrome Associated with Maternal Postpartum Hemorrhage," *Journal of Human Lactation* 11, 2 (1995): 123–26.

10 W.I. Thomas, "The Relation of Research to the Social Process," in *W.I. Thomas on Social Organization and Social Personality: Selected Papers*, ed. Morris Janowitz (Chicago: University of Chicago Press, 1966), 301.

11 Nancy P. Chin, "Environmental Toxins: Physical, Social, and Emotional," *Breastfeeding Medicine* 5, 5 (2010): 223–24.

12 Julie A. Hilson, Kathleen M. Rasmussen, and Chris L. Kjolhede, "Maternal Obesity and Breast-Feeding Success in a Rural Population of White Women," *American Journal of Clinical Nutrition* 66, 6 (1997): 1271–78; Kathleen M. Rasmussen, Julie A. Hilson, and Chris L. Kjolhede, "Obesity May Impair Lactogenesis II," *Journal of Nutrition* 131, 11 (2001): 3009S–11S; Peter Hartmann and Mark Cregan, "Lactogenesis and the Effects of Insulin-Dependent Diabetes Mellitus and Prematurity," *Journal of Nutrition* 131, 11 (2001): 3016S–20S.

13 Nova Scotia, Breastfeeding in Nova Scotia: Responsibilities of the Nova Scotia Department of Health and the Nova Scotia Department of Health Promotion and Protection, policy statement, last modified June 2006, https://novascotia.ca/dhw/healthy-communities/documents/Provincial-Breastfeeding-Policy.pdf.

14 The Seven Point Plan is elaborated in Breastfeeding Committee for Canada, *Breastfeeding Statement of the Breastfeeding Commitee for Canada,* 2002, http://www.breastfeedingcanada.ca/documents/webdoc5.pdf.

15 Healthy Eating Action Group of the Nova Scotia Alliance for Healthy Eating and Physical Activity, *Healthy Eating Nova Scotia,* policy document produced in partnership with the Office of Health Promotion, March 2005, https://novascotia.ca/dhw/healthy-communities/documents/Provincial-Healthy-Eating-Strategy.pdf.

16 WHO/UNICEF, *Protecting, Promoting and Supporting Breast-Feeding: The Special Role of Maternity Services,* Geneva, Switzerland, https://www.who.int/nutrition/publications/infantfeeding/9241561300/en/.

17 Lise Dubois et al., "Family Food Insufficiency Is Related to Overweight among Preschoolers," *Social Science and Medicine* 63, 6 (2006): 1503–16.

18 Kathryn E. McIsaac, David C. Stocky, and Wendy Lou, "Household Food Security and Breast-Feeding Duration among Canadian Inuit," *Public Health Nutrition* 20, 1 (2017): 64–71, https://doi.org/10.1017/S136898001600166X.

19 Sarah Orr et al., "Relation between Household Food Insecurity and Breastfeeding in Canada," *Canadian Medical Association Journal* 190, 11 (2018): E312–19, https://doi.org/10.1503/cmaj.170880.

20 Martha Morrow and Simon Barraclough, "Breast-Feeding and Public Policy in Australia: Limitation of a Nutritional Focus," *Health Promotion International* 8, 2 (1993): 135.

21 Deborah McCarter-Spaulding, "Is Breastfeeding Fair? Tensions in Feminist Perspectives on Breastfeeding and the Family," *Journal of Human Lactation* 24, 2 (2008): 211.

22 Elizabeth Dowler, "Food and Health Inequalities: The Challenge for Sustaining Just Consumption," *Local Environment* 13, 8 (2008): 761.

23 Ibid.; Elizabeth Dowler, "Policy Initiatives to Address Low-Income Households' Nutritional Needs in the UK," *Proceedings of the Nutrition Society* 67, 3 (2008): 289–300; Anne Murcott, "Nutrition and Inequalities: A Note on Sociological Approaches," *European Journal of Public Health* 12, 3 (2002): 203–7.

24 Vanessa Maher, *The Anthropology of Breast-Feeding: Natural Law or Social Construct* (Providence, RI: Berg Publishers, 1992), 153.

Chapter 4: The Bottle for Baby

1 Various studies of infant feeding in low-income circumstances identify this concern. See Catherine J. Mackereth and Susan J. Milner, "The Influence of Family Culture on Eating in Low Income Families," *British Food Journal* 109, 3 (2007): 198–205; M. Jane Heinig and Kathryn G. Dewey, "Health Effects of Breast Feeding for Mothers: A Critical Review," *Nutrition Research Reviews* 10, 1 (1997): 35–56, https://doi.org/10.1079/NRR19970004.

2 R. Lakshman, D. Ogilvie, and K.K. Ong, "Mothers' Experiences of Bottle-Feeding: A Systematic Review of Qualitative and Quantitative Studies," *Archives of Disease in Childhood* 94, 8 (2009): 596–601.

3 Angela noted that the cost of specialty infant formula could be partially covered by income assistance, but only if a nutritionist determined that there was a need for it.

4 "About WIC," United States Department of Agriculture, Food and Nutrition Service, last modified October 10, 2013, https://www.fns.usda.gov/wic/about-wic.

5 "Healthy Start," National Health Service, accessed April 17, 2017, https://www.healthystart.nhs.uk.

6 Public Health Agency of Canada, *The Canada Prenatal Nutrition Program: A Decade of Promoting the Health of Mothers, Babies and Communities* (Ottawa: Minister of Health, 2007).

7 See George Kent, "WIC's Promotion of Infant Formula in the United States," *International Breastfeeding Journal* 1, 8 (2006): n.p., https://doi.org/10.1186/1746-4358-1-8; Public Health Agency of Canada, *Protecting, Promoting and Supporting Breastfeeding: A Practical Workbook for Community-Based Programs*, 2nd ed. (Ottawa: Public Health Agency of Canada, 2014), http://www.phac-aspc.gc.ca/hp-ps/dca-dea/publications/pdf/ppsb-ppsam-eng.pdf.

8 Rosalie Chappell, *Social Welfare in Canadian Society*, 4th ed. (Toronto: Nelson Education, 2010). Policy steering is akin to Michel Foucault's concept of governmentality, which is concerned with the "techniques and procedures for directing human behavior" (*Ethics: Subjectivity and Truth: Essential Works of Michel Foucault 1954–1984* [New York: The New Press, 1997, 82]) by governing from afar, typical of neoliberal societies in which power is decentralized. In "Governmentality" (*The Foucault Effect: Studies in Governmentality*, edited by Graham Burchell, Colin Gordon, and Peter Miller [Hemel Hempstead, UK: Harvester Wheatsheaf, 1991]), Foucault argued that discourses are used instead of coercive force to impose order on a social group. In this sense, discourses serve as a mechanism directing behaviour in which the self is governed by the self.

9 The guide is now available on the Government of Nova Scotia website: Parent Health Education Resource Working Group, *How to Feed Your Baby with Infant Formula* (Halifax: Nova Scotia Department of Health and Wellness, 2015), https://novascotia.ca.

10 World Health Organization (WHO), *International Code of Marketing of Breast-Milk Substitutes* (Geneva: WHO, 1981), http://www.who.int/nutrition/publications/code_english.pdf.

11 Breastfeeding Committee for Canada, *BCC BFI Ten Steps and WHO Code Outcome Indicators* (2017), http://www.breastfeedingcanada.ca.

12 Anne Murcott, "Purity and Pollution: Body Management and the Social Place of Infancy," in *Body Matters: Essays on the Sociology of the Body*, ed. Sue Scott and David Morgan (Bristol, PA: Falmer Press, 1993), 135.

13 Some mothers and policy/program interviewees discussed donor breast milk and peer-to-peer sharing of breast milk as a means to access food. Mothers had mixed feelings about using breast milk from others. The family resource worker/lactation consultant indicated that there was little support for formalized human milk sharing through milk banks and suggested that government health employees seemed uncomfortable about informal milk-sharing practice. While access to breast milk might be a particularly helpful alternative for food insecure households, access to third-party breast milk is rare, unregulated, and contested. Canada currently has just four human milk banks – in Vancouver, Calgary, Montreal, and Toronto – and the milk is reserved primarily for premature or sick babies. Informal human milk sharing, such as that facilitated by the Facebook group Human Milk 4 Human Babies, has been the subject of advisories by the Canadian Pediatric Society and Health Canada (J.H. Kim and S. Unger, "Human Milk Banking," Canadian Pediatric Society, Nutrition and Gastroenterology Committee position statement, November 1, 2010, reaffirmed February 28, 2018, https://www.cps.ca/en/documents/position/human-milk-banking; "Health Canada Raises Concern about the Use of Unprocessed Human Milk," Health Canada, November 25, 2010, http://www.healthycanadians.gc.ca/recall-alert-rappel-avis/hc-sc/2010/13461a-eng.php. Both have released policy positions stating that accessing human milk outside of regulated milk banks is risky due to a lack of donor screening and pasteurization. Infact Canada countered by arguing that Health Canada's advisory lacked a basis in science ("Mother's Milk and Safe Milk Sharing: Health Canada's Advisory Lacks Scientific Basis," Infact Canada, December 7, 2010, http://www.infactcanada.ca/whatsnew/milk-sharing.html).

14 Public Health Agency of Canada, *Protecting, Promoting and Supporting Breastfeeding*, 18, emphasis in original.

15 The Nova Scotia Volunteer Services Act, under the provision of "food or sundries to person in need," protects a volunteer from being liable for "damages incurred as a result of injury, illness, disease or death resulting from the consumption of food or the use of sundries

by a person in need unless it is established that (a) the injury, illness, disease or death was caused by the gross negligence or the wilful misconduct of the volunteer; or (b) the volunteer knew that the food or sundries were contaminated or otherwise unfit for human consumption or use at the time of donation or distribution, respectively" (https://nslegislature.ca/legislative-business/bills-statutes/consolidated-public-statutes).

16 I indicated that I had never heard of any special grants other than the special diet allowance for income assistance recipients to support purchases of specialized formulas.

17 "Food Banks and Infant Formula," Infact Canada, December 9, 2005, http://www.infactcanada.ca/Action_Alert_Dec9_05.htm.

18 Kenneth Rosenberg et al., "Marketing Infant Formula through Hospitals: The Impact of Commercial Hospital Discharge Packs on Breastfeeding," *American Journal of Public Health* 98, 2 (2008): 290–95.

19 WHO, *International Code of Marketing of Breast-Milk Substitutes* (Geneva: WHO, 1981), http://www.who.int/nutrition/publications/code_english.pdf.

20 "Sample Letter to Food Banks Canada Warning against Their Dangerous Partnership with Nestlé," Infact Canada, n.d., http://infactcanada.ca/food-banks-canada-nestle-letter.html.

21 Janet Poppendieck, *Sweet Charity? Emergency Food and the End of Entitlement* (New York: Penguin, 1998); Graham Riches, *Food Bank Nations: Poverty, Corporate Charity and the Right to Food* (New York: Routledge, 2018).

22 For full results see, Lesley Frank, "Finding Formula: Community-Based Organizational Responses to Infant Formula Needs Due to Household Food Insecurity," *Canadian Food Studies Journal* 5, 1 (2018): 90–112.

23 In fact, a few food banks indicated that they would give infant formula only to mothers. In one case, the staff refused to give it to men because they used it to 'cut' cocaine in the local area; in another, staff would not give formula to anyone indicating that they were babysitting the infant; i.e., grandparents.

24 "Ethical Foodbanking Code," Food Banks Canada, n.d., https://www.foodbankscanada.ca/Our-Work/Ethical-Foodbanking-Code.aspx (emphasis added).

25 Health Canada, *Nutrition for Healthy Term Infant* (Ottawa: Minister of Health, last modified August 18, 2015), https://www.canada.ca/en/health-canada/services/canada-food-guide/resources/infant-feeding/nutrition-healthy-term-infants-recommendations-birth-six-months.html.

26 World Health Organization (WHO), *International Code of Marketing of Breast-Milk Substitutes.*

27 Penny Van Esterik, "Right to Food, Right to Feed, Right to be Fed: The Intersection of Women's Rights and the Right to Food," *Agriculture and Human Values* 16, 2 (1999): 225–32.

Conclusion

1 "Trends in Breastfeeding Practices in Canada (2001 to 2009–2010)," Health Canada, last modified April 24, 2012, http://www.hc-sc.gc.ca/fn-an/surveill/nutrition/commun/prenatal/trends-tendances-eng.php.

2 Group aggregate statistics on breastfeeding cluster together what might be very different culturally based infant feeding histories and preferences. As well, nutrition surveillance statistics capture only a limited aspect of infant feeding practices: *breastfeeding initiation* includes trying to breastfeed even for a short time, while *exclusive breastfeeding* excludes those who almost exclusively breastfeed or use mixed feeding strategies. No Canadian statistics capture formula feeding practices. We do not know the extent to which Canadian mothers, even those who breastfeed, rely on formula to feed their babies.

3 World Health Organization (WHO), *International Code of Marketing of Breast-Milk Substitutes* (Geneva: WHO, 1981), http://www.who.int/nutrition/publications/code_english.pdf.

4 Stephen Brooks and Lydia Miljan, *Public Policy in Canada: An Introduction* (Don Mills, ON: Oxford University Press, 2003).

5 Gøsta Esping-Anderson, *The Three Worlds of Welfare Capitalism* (Princeton, NJ: Princeton University Press, 1990).

6 Michel Foucault, *History of Sexuality*, vol. 3, *The Care of the Self* (London: Penguin, 1990); JaneMaree Maher, Suzanne Frazer, and Jo Lindsay, "Between Provisioning and Consuming? Children, Mothers and 'Childhood Obesity,'" *Health Sociology Review* 19, 3 (2010): 304–16.

7 Nova Scotia Department of Agriculture, "Tax Credit Supports Farmer Donations to Food Banks," news release, May 19, 2016, https://novascotia.ca/news/release/?id=20160519005.

8 Graham Riches, *Food Bank Nations: Poverty, Corporate Charity and the Right to Food* (New York: Routledge, 2018).

9 She noted that she also learned from researchers like me and thought it was her role to facilitate strategic dissemination of this research within her policy domains: "We need to be working with folks like you that are doing important things to make things credible, connected to reality; you are our lifeline, too, because I have very limited power."

10 United Nations, *Convention on the Rights of the Child*, adopted by General Assembly Resolution 44/25, November 20, 1989, https://www.ohchr.org/en/professionalinterest/pages/crc.aspx.

11 Patricia L. Williams et al., "Affordability of a Nutritious Diet for Income Assistance Recipients in Nova Scotia (2002–2010)," *Canadian Journal of Public Health* 103, 3 (2012): 183–88; Patricia L. Williams et al., "'I Would Have Never Thought That I Would Be in Such a Predicament': Voices from Women Experiencing Food Insecurity in Nova Scotia, Canada," *Journal of Hunger and Environmental Nutrition* 7, 2–3 (2012): 253–70.

12 David Macdonald, *A Policymaker's Guide to Basic Income,* Canadian Centre for Policy Alternatives (CCPA) Reports and Studies (Ottawa: CCPA, October 2016), https://www.policyalternatives.ca.

13 Statistics Canada, "Low Income Statistics by Age, Sex and Economic Family Type," Table 11-10-013501, https://www150.statcan.gc.ca/t1/tbl1/en/cv.action?pid=1110013501.

14 Statistics Canada, *Census in Brief: Children Living in Low-Income Households,* Catalogue no. 98-200-X2016012 (Ottawa: Statistics Canada, 2017), http://www12.statcan.gc.ca/census-recensement/2016/as-sa/98-200-x/2016012/98-200-x2016012-eng.cfm.

15 George Kent, "Child Feeding and Human Rights," *International Breastfeeding Journal* 1, 27 (2006): n.p.

Appendix: Anatomy of the Study

1 For methodological details, see Lesley Frank, "Finding Formula: Community-Based Organizational Responses to Infant Formula Needs Due to Household Food Insecurity," *Canadian Food Studies Journal* 5, 1 (2018): 90–112.

2 Judith M. Newman, "Action Research: A Brief Overview," *Forum: Qualitative Social Research* 1, 1 (2000), http://qualitative-research.net/fqs-texte/1-00/1-00newman-e.htm.

3 B. Poland et al., "The Social Context of Smoking: The Next Frontier in Tobacco Control?" *Tobacco Control* 15, 1 (2006): 60.

4 Treena Delormier, Katherine L. Frohlich, and Louise Potvin, "Food and Eating as Social Practice: Understanding Eating Patterns as Social Phenomena and Implications for Public Health," *Sociology of Health and Illness* 31, 2 (2009): 215–28.

5 Alan Warde, *The Practice of Eating* (Cambridge: Polity Press, 2016), 50.

6 For a methodological reflection see, Lesley Frank, "Reflections of a Food Studies Researcher: Connecting the Community-University-Policy Divide … Becoming the Hyphens!" *Canadian Food Studies Journal* 1, 1 (2014): 88–98.

7 Norman K. Denzin and Yvonna S. Lincoln, "Introduction: The Discipline and Practice of Qualitative Research," in *The SAGE Handbook of Qualitative Research,* 5th ed., ed. Norman K. Denzin and Yvonna S. Lincoln (Thousand Oaks, CA: Sage Publications, 2018), 1–26; Robert K. Yin, *Case Study Research: Design and Methods,* 5th ed. (Thousand Oaks, CA: Sage Publications, 2014), 3–26.

8 "Trends in Breastfeeding Practices in Canada (2001 to 2009–2010)," Health Canada, last modified April 24, 2012, http://www.hc-sc.gc.ca/fn-an/surveill/nutrition/commun/prenatal/trends-tendances-eng.php; Valerie Tarasuk, Andy Mitchell, and Naomi Dachner, *Household Food Insecurity in Canada, 2014* (Toronto: Research to Identify Policy Options to Reduce Food Insecurity [PROOF], 2016), https://proof.utoronto.ca.

9 Kristin G. Esterberg, *Qualitative Methods in Social Research* (Toronto: McGraw-Hill, 2002), 158; Anselm Strauss and Juliet Corbin, *Basics of Qualitative Research: Grounded Theory Procedures and Techniques*, 4th ed. (Newbury Park, CA: Sage, 2017).

10 John W. Creswell and J. David Creswell, *Research Design: Qualitative, Quantitative, and Mixed Methods Approaches*, 5th ed. (Thousand Oaks, CA: Sage Publications, 2018), 245–46.

11 Statistics Canada, "Crude Birth Rate, Age-Specific Fertility Rates and Total Fertility Rates (Live Births)," Table 13-10-0418-01, https://doi.org/10.25318/1310041801-eng.

12 Nova Scotia Community Counts, "Browse Data by Geography," accessed August 24, 2012, https://novascotia.ca.

13 Statistics Canada, "Selected Income Characteristics of Census Families by Family Type," CANSIM Table 11-10-0009-01, accessed January 18, 2020, https://www150.statcan.gc.ca.

14 The Canada Child Tax Benefit (CCTB) consisted of a monthly payment that combined federal and provincial government transfers: the National Child Benefit (NCB), the National Child Benefit Supplement (NCBS) for low-income families, and the Nova Scotia Child Benefit. See *The National Child Benefit: Progress Report 2007*, Catalogue no. HS1-3/2007-1 (Ottawa: Government of Canada, 2008), http://publications.gc.ca/collections/collection_2013/rhdcc-hrsdc/HS1-3-2007-1-eng.pdf; "Nova Scotia Child Benefit," last modified July 4, 2012, https://novascotia.ca/coms/families/ChildBenefit.html. In July 2016, the new Canada Child Benefit came into effect, replacing the NCB and NCBS. The Universal Child Care Benefit, introduced in 2006, was a monthly payment to all families with children under the age of six to help cover the cost of child care. In 2015, the UCCB increased from $100 to $160 per month for each child younger than six. It was also expanded to include children six to seventeen, paying a monthly benefit of $60 per child. The program was discontinued when the new Canada Child Benefit was implemented in 2016.

Bibliography

Alaimo, Katherine, Christine M. Olson, Edward A. Frongillo, and Ronette R. Briefel. "Food Insufficiency, Family Income, and Health in US Preschool and School-Aged Children." *American Journal of Public Health* 91, 5 (2001): 781–86.

Allen, L. "Maternal Micronutrient Malnutrition: Effects on Breast Milk and Infant Nutrition, and Priorities for Intervention." *SCN News* 11 (1994): 21–24.

Anderson, S.A. "Core Indicators of Nutritional State for Difficult-to-Sample Populations." *Journal of Nutrition* 120 (1990): 1559–600.

Andrée, Peter, Lynn Langille, Chantal Clement, Patricia Williams, and Emily Norgang. "Structural Constraints and Enablers to Community Food Security in Nova Scotia, Canada." *Journal of Hunger and Environmental Nutrition* 11, 4 (2016): 456–90.

Baker, Maureen. "Child Poverty, Maternal Health and Social Benefits." *Current Sociology* 50, 6 (2002): 823–83.

Ball, Thomas M., and Anne L. Wright. "Health Care Costs of Formula-Feeding in the First Year of Life." *Pediatrics* 103, 4, part 2 (1999): 870–76.

Barker, D.J.P. "The Developmental Origins of Adult Disease." *Journal of the American College of Nutrition* 23, supplement 6 (2004): 588S–95S.

BC Centre for Disease Control. *Food Costing in BC 2017: Assessing the Affordability of Healthy Eating*. Vancouver: Centre for Disease Control, Population and Public Health Program, 2018. http://www.bccdc.ca/pop-public-health/Documents/food-costing-BC-2017.pdf.

Beagan, Brenda, Gwen E. Chapman, Andrea D'Sylva, and B. Raewyn Bassett. "'It's Just Easier for Me to Do It': Rationalizing the Family Division of Foodwork." *Sociology* 42, 4 (2008): 653–71.

Beaumier, Maude C., and James D. Ford. "Food Insecurity among Inuit Women Exacerbated by Socio-Economic Stresses and Climate Change." *Canadian Journal of Public Health* 101, 3 (2010): 196–201.

Bertmann, Farryl M.W., and Amy L. Yaroch. "Role of Breast Milk and Breastfeeding within the Context of a Sustainable, Resilient Food System." *Journal of Hunger and Environmental Nutrition* 11, 2 (2016): 242–53.

Bezanson, Kate. "The Neo-Liberal State and Social Reproduction: Gender and Household Insecurity in the Late 1990s." In *Social Reproduction: Feminist Political Economy Challenges Neo-Liberalism,* edited by Kate Bezanson and Meg Luxton, 173–214. Montreal and Kingston: McGill-Queen's University Press, 2006.

Bonyata, Kelly. "Do Breastfeeding Mothers Need Extra Calories or Fluids?" *KellyMom.* Last modified March 10, 2019. http://kellymom.com/nutrition/mothers-diet/mom-calories-fluids.

Borders, Ann E. Bryant, William A. Grobman, Laura B. Amsden, and Jane L. Holl. "Chronic Stress and Low Birth Weight Neonates in a Low-Income Population of Women." *Obstetrics and Gynecology* 109, 2, part 1 (2007): 331–38.

Bourdieu, Pierre. *Distinction: A Social Critique of the Judgement of Taste.* Translated by Richard Nice. Cambridge, MA: Harvard University Press, 1984.

Braedley, Susan. "Someone to Watch over You: Gender, Class, and Social Reproduction." In *Social Reproduction: Feminist Political Economy Challenges Neo-Liberalism,* edited by Kate Bezanson and Meg Luxton, 215–30. Montreal and Kingston: McGill-Queen's University Press, 2006.

Brooks, Stephen, and Lydia Miljan. *Public Policy in Canada: An Introduction.* Don Mills, ON: Oxford University Press, 2003.

Butte, Nancy F., Mardia G. López-Alarcón, and Cutberto Garza. *Nutrient Adequacy of Exclusive Breastfeeding for the Term Infant during the First Six Months of Life.* Geneva: World Health Organization, 2002.

Cairns, Kate, and Josée Johnson. *Food and Femininity.* New York: Bloomsbury, 2015.

Campbell, Cathy C., and Ellen Desjardins. "A Model and Research Approach for Studying the Management of Limited Food Resources by Low Income Families." *Journal of Nutrition Education and Behavior* 21, 4 (1989): 162–71.

Canada. Department of Agriculture and Agri-Food. *Canada's Action Plan for Food Security.* Report produced in response to the World Food Summit Plan for Action, 1998. http://www.agr.gc.ca/misb/fsec-seca/pdf/action_e.pdf.

Chappell, Rosalie. *Social Welfare in Canadian Society.* 4th ed. Toronto: Nelson Education, 2010.

Charles, Nickie, and Marion Kerr. "Food for Feminist Thought." *Sociological Review* 34, 3 (1986): 537–72.

–. *Women, Food, and Families.* Manchester: Manchester University Press, 1988.

Chen, J., and J. Che. "Food Insecurity in Canadian Households." *Health Reports* 12, 4 (2001): 11–22.

Chin, Nancy P. "Environmental Toxins: Physical, Social, and Emotional." *Breastfeeding Medicine* 5, 5 (2010): 223–24.

Cook, John T., Deborah A. Frank, Carol Berkowitz, Maureen M. Black, Patrick H. Casey, Diana B. Cutts, Alan F. Meyers, Nieves Zaldivar, Anne Skalicky, Suzette Levenson, Tim Heeren, and Mark Nord. "Food Insecurity Is Associated with Adverse Health Outcomes among Human Infants and Toddlers." *Journal of Nutrition* 134, 6 (2004): 1432–38.

Counihan, Carole M. *Around the Tuscan Table: Food, Family, and Gender in Twentieth-Century Florence.* New York: Routledge, 2004.

Creswell, John W., and J. David Creswell. *Research Design: Qualitative, Quantitative, and Mixed Methods Approaches*, 5th ed. Thousand Oaks, CA: Sage Publications, 2018.

Davis, Barbara, and Valerie Tarasuk. "Hunger in Canada." *Agriculture and Human Values* 11, 4 (1994): 50–57.

Delormier, Treena, Katherine L. Frohlich, and Louise Potvin. "Food and Eating as Social Practice: Understanding Eating Patterns as Social Phenomena and Implications for Public Health." *Sociology of Health and Illness* 31, 2 (2009): 215–28.

Denzin, Norman K., and Yvonna S. Lincoln. "Introduction: The Discipline and Practice of Qualitative Research." In *The SAGE Handbook of Qualitative Research*, 5th ed., edited by Norman K. Denzin and Yvonna S. Lincoln, 1–17. Thousand Oaks, CA: Sage Publications, 2018.

DeVault, Marjorie L. *Feeding the Family: The Social Organization of Caring as Gendered Work.* Chicago: University of Chicago Press, 1991.

Devine, Carol M., Margaret M. Connors, Jeffrey Sobal, and Carole A. Bisogni. "Sandwiching It In: Spillover of Work onto Food Choices and Family Roles in Low- and Moderate-Income Urban Households." *Social Science and Medicine* 56, 3 (2003): 617–30.

Dewey, Kathryn G. "Energy and Protein Requirements during Lactation." *Annual Review of Nutrition* 17 (1997): 19–36.

Dowler, Elizabeth. "Food and Health Inequalities: The Challenge for Sustaining Just Consumption." *Local Environment* 13, 8 (2008): 759–72.

–. "Policy Initiatives to Address Low-Income Households' Nutritional Needs in the UK." *Proceedings of the Nutrition Society* 67, 3 (2008): 289–300.

Draper, Susan B. "Breast-Feeding as a Sustainable Resource System." *American Anthropologist* 98, 2 (1996): 258–65.

Dubois, Lise, Anna Farmer, Manon Girard, and Marion Porcherie. "Family Food Insufficiency Is Related to Overweight among Preschoolers." *Social Science and Medicine* 63, 6 (2006): 1503–16.

Esping-Anderson, Gøsta. *The Three Worlds of Welfare Capitalism.* Princeton, NJ: Princeton University Press, 1990.

Esterberg, Kristin G. *Qualitative Methods in Social Research.* Toronto: McGraw-Hill, 2002.

Evans, Patricia. "Eroding Canadian Social Welfare: The Mulroney Legacy, 1984–1993." In *Social Fabric or Patchwork Quilt: The Development of Social Policy in Canada,* edited by Raymond B. Black and Jeffrey A. Keshen, 263–74. Toronto: Broadview Press, 2006.

Fildes, Valerie. "The Culture and Biology of Breastfeeding: An Historical Review of Western Europe." In *Breastfeeding: Biocultural Perspectives,* edited by Patricia Stuart-Macadam and Katherine A. Dettwyler, 101–27. New York: Aldine De Gruyter, 1995.

Food and Agriculture Organization (FAO). *Rome Declaration on World Food Security and World Food Summit Plan of Action.* Rome: FAO, 1996.

Food and Agriculture Organization and the World Health Organization (FAO and WHO). Enterobacter Sakazakii *and Other Microorganisms in Powdered Infant Formula.* Microbiological Risk Assessment Series no. 6, meeting report. Geneva: FAO/WHO, 2004.

Ford, James D., and Maude Beaumier. "Feeding the Family during Times of Stress: Experience and Determinants of Food Insecurity in an Inuit Community." *Geographical Journal* 177, 1 (2011): 44–61.

Foucault, Michel. *Ethics: Subjectivity and Truth.* Edited by Paul Rabinow. Translated by Robert Hurley et al. New York: The New Press, 1997.

–. "Governmentality." In *The Foucault Effect: Studies in Governmentality,* edited by Graham Burchell, Colin Gordon, and Peter Miller, 87–104. Hemel Hempstead, UK: Harvester Wheatsheaf, 1991.

–. *History of Sexuality.* Vol. 3, *The Care of the Self.* London: Penguin, 1990.

Frank, Lesley. "The Breastfeeding Paradox: A Critique of Policy Related to Infant Food Insecurity in Canada." *Food, Culture and Society* 8, 1 (2015): 107–29.

–. "Exploring Infant Feeding Practices in Food Insecure Households: What Is the Real Issue?" *Food and Foodways: Explorations in the History and Culture of Human Nourishment* 23, 3 (2015): 186–209.

–. "Finding Formula: Community-Based Organizational Responses to Infant Formula Needs Due to Household Food Insecurity." *Canadian Food Studies Journal* 5, 1 (2018): 90–112.

–. "Reflections of a Food Studies Researcher: Connecting the Community-University-Policy Divide … Becoming the Hyphens!" *Canadian Food Studies Journal* 1, 1 (2014): 88–98.

Friendly, Abigail. *Towards Food Security Policy for Canada's Social Housing Sector.* Canadian Policy Research Networks Research Report. Ottawa: Canadian Social Policy Research Networks and Social Housing Services Corporation, 2008.

Government of Canada. *The National Child Benefit: Progress Report 2007,* Catalogue no. HS1-3/2007-1 (Ottawa: Government of Canada, 2008), http://publications.gc.ca/collections/collection_2013/rhdcc-hrsdc/HS1-3-2007-1-eng.pdf.

Greiner, Ted. "Beyond Melamine: More Reasons Not to Use Animal Milk in Infant Feeding." *Journal of Human Lactation* 25, 4 (2009): 397–99.

Hamelin, Anne-Marie, Micheline Beaudry, and Jean-Pierre Habicht. "Characterization of Household Food Insecurity in Québec: Food and Feelings." *Social Science and Medicine* 54, 1 (2002): 119–32.

Hartmann, Peter, and Mark Cregan. "Lactogenesis and the Effects of Insulin-Dependent Diabetes Mellitus and Prematurity." *Journal of Nutrition* 131, 11 (2001): 3016S–20S.

Hausman, Bernice L. *Mother's Milk: Breastfeeding Controversies in American Culture.* New York: Routledge, 2003.

Health Canada. *Exclusive Breastfeeding Duration: 2004 Health Canada Recommendation*. Publication no. 4824. Ottawa: Health Canada, 2004. https://www.healthstandnutrition.com/wp-content/uploads/2011/09/2004-Health-Canada-exclusive-breastfeeding-duration.pdf.

Healthy Eating Action Group of the Nova Scotia Alliance for Healthy Eating and Physical Activity. *Healthy Eating Nova Scotia*. Policy document produced in partnership with the Office of Health Promotion. March 2005. https://novascotia.ca/dhw/healthy-communities/documents/Provincial-Healthy-Eating-Strategy.pdf.

Heinig, M. Jane, and Kathryn G. Dewey. "Health Effects of Breast Feeding for Mothers: A Critical Review." *Nutrition Research Reviews* 10, 1 (1997): 35–56. https://doi.org/10.1079/NRR19970004.

Hernandez, Daphne C., and Alison Jacknowitz. "Transient, but not Persistent, Adult Food Insecurity Influences Toddler Development." *Journal of Nutrition* 139, 8 (2009): 1517–24.

Hilson, Julie A., Kathleen M. Rasmussen, and Chris L. Kjolhede. "Maternal Obesity and Breast-Feeding Success in a Rural Population of White Women." *American Journal of Clinical Nutrition* 66, 6 (1997): 1271–78.

Hobbs, Karen, Wayne MacEachern, Ann McIvor, and Steve Turner. "Waste of a Nation: Poor People Speak Out about Charity." *Canadian Review of Social Policy* 31 (1993): 94–104.

Huffman, S.L., E. Rasmusson, V. Newman, and C. O'Gara. *Breastfeeding: A Natural Resource for Food Security*. USAID Cooperative Agreement no. DPE-5966-A-00-1045-00. Washington, DC: Wellstart International, 1992.

Infact Canada. *Breastfeeding and Food Security: The High Cost of Formula Feeding.* Rockport, ON: Infact Canada, 2004. http://www.infactcanada.ca/Breastfeeding_and_Food_Security.pdf.

–. "The Cost of Formula and Infant Feeding Security." *INFACT Canada Newsletter* (Fall 1997): n.p. http://www.infactcanada.ca/security.htm.

Jacobs-Starkey, Linda, Harriet V. Kuhnlein, and Katherine Gray-Donald. "Food Bank Users: Sociodemographic and Nutritional Characteristics." *Canadian Medical Association Journal* 158, 9 (1998): 1143–49.

Jelliffe, D.B., and E.F.P. Jelliffe. *Human Milk in the Modern World*. Oxford: Oxford University Press, 1978.

Julier, Alice P. *Eating Together: Food, Friendship, and Inequality*. Urbana: University of Illinois Press, 2013.

Kent, George. "Child Feeding and Human Rights." *International Breastfeeding Journal* 1, 27 (2006): n.p. https://doi:10.1186/1746-4358-1-27.

–. "WIC's Promotion of Infant Formula in the United States." *International Breastfeeding Journal* 1, 8 (2006): n.p. https://doi.org/10.1186/1746-4358-1-8.

Kent, Jacqueline C., Danielle K. Prime, and Catherine P. Garbin. "Principles for Maintaining or Increasing Breast Milk Production." *Journal of Obstetric, Gynecologic, and Neonatal Nursing* 41, 1 (2012): 114–21.

Kim, J.H., and S. Unger. "Human Milk Banking." Canadian Pediatric Society, Nutrition and Gastroenterology Committee position statement, November 1, 2010, reaffirmed February 2-18. https://www.cps.ca/en/documents/position/human-milk-banking.

Kirkpatrick, Sharon I., Lynn McIntyre, and Melissa L. Potestio. "Child Hunger and Long-Term Adverse Consequences for Health." *Archives of Pediatrics and Adolescent Medicine* 164, 8 (2010): 754–62.

Kirkpatrick, Sharon I., and Valerie Tarasuk. "Adequacy of Food Spending Is Related to Housing Expenditures among Lower-Income Canadian Households." *Public Health Nutrition* 10, 12 (2007): 1464–73.

Kominiarek, Michelle, and Priya Rajan. "Nutrition Recommendations in Pregnancy and Lactation." *Medical Clinics of North America* 100, 6 (2016): 1199–215.

Lakshman, R., D. Ogilvie, and K.K. Ong. "Mothers' Experiences of Bottle-Feeding: A Systematic Review of Qualitative and Quantitative Studies." *Archives of Disease in Childhood* 94, 8 (2009): 596–601.

Lawrence, Ruth A. "The Eradication of Poverty One Child at a Time through Breastfeeding: A Contribution to the Global Theme Issue on Poverty and Human Development." *Breastfeeding Medicine* 2, 4 (2007): 193–94.

Macdonald, David. *A Policymaker's Guide to Basic Income*. Canadian Centre for Policy Alternatives (CCPA) Reports and Studies. Ottawa: CCPA, October 2016. https://www.policyalternatives.ca.

Mackereth, Catherine J., and Susan J. Milner. "The Influence of Family Culture on Eating in Low Income Families." *British Food Journal* 109, 3 (2007): 198–205.

Mah, Catherine L., Catherine Hamill, Krista Rondeau, and Lynn McIntyre. "A Frame-Critical Policy Analysis of Canada's Response to World Food Summit 1998–2008." *Archives of Public Health* 72, 41 (2014): 1–7.

Maher, JaneMaree, Suzanne Frazer, and Jo Lindsay. "Between Provisioning and Consuming? Children, Mothers and 'Childhood Obesity.'" *Health Sociology Review* 19, 3 (2010): 304–16.

Maher, Vanessa. *The Anthropology of Breast-Feeding: Natural Law or Social Construct.* Providence, RI: Berg Publishers, 1992.

Mammen, Sheila, Jean W. Bauer, and Leslie Richards. "Understanding Persistent Food Insecurity: A Paradox of Place and Circumstance." *Social Indicators Research* 92 (2009): 151–68.

Martorell, Reynaldo. "Improved Nutrition in the First 1000 Days and Adult Human Capital and Health." *American Journal of Human Biology* 29, 2 (2017): e22952. https://doi.org/10.1002/ajhb.22952.

McCarter-Spaulding, Deborah. "Is Breastfeeding Fair? Tensions in Feminist Perspectives on Breastfeeding and the Family." *Journal of Human Lactation* 24, 2 (2008): 206–12.

McIntyre, Lynn, Theresa Glanville, Kim Raine, Jutta Dayle, Bonnie Anderson, and Noreen Battaglia. "Do Low-Income Lone Mothers Compromise Their Nutrition to Feed Their Children?" *Canadian Medical Association Journal* 168 (2003): 686–91.

McIntyre, Lynn, Jeanne V.A. Williams, Dina H. Lavorato, and Scott Patten. "Depression and Suicide Ideation in Late Adolescence and Early Adulthood Are an Outcome of Child Hunger." *Journal of Affective Disorders* 150, 1 (2013): 123–29.

McIsaac, Kathryn E., David C. Stocky, and Wendy Lou. "Household Food Security and Breast-Feeding Duration among Canadian Inuit." *Public Health Nutrition* 20, 1 (2017): 64–71. https://doi.org/10.1017/S136898001600166X.

McKay, Lindsey, Sophie Mathieu, and Andrea Doucet. "Parental-Leave Rich and Parental-Leave Poor: Inequality in Canadian Labour Market Based Leave Policies." *Journal of Industrial Relations* 58, 4 (2016): 543–62.

Mirowsky, John, and Catherine E. Ross. "Economic Hardship across the Life Course." *American Sociological Review* 64, 4 (1999): 548–69.

Morrow, Martha, and Simon Barraclough. "Breast-Feeding and Public Policy in Australia: Limitation of a Nutritional Focus." *Health Promotion International* 8, 2 (1993): 135–46.

Murcott, Anne. "Family Meals – A Thing of the Past?" In *Food, Health and Identity,* edited by Pat Caplan, 32–50. New York: Routledge, 1997.

–. "Nutrition and Inequalities: A Note on Sociological Approaches." *European Journal of Public Health* 12, 3 (2002): 203–7.

–. "Purity and Pollution: Body Management and the Social Place of Infancy." In *Body Matters: Essays on the Sociology of the Body,* edited by Sue Scott and David Morgan, 122–34. Bristol, PA: Falmer Press, 1993.

Nathoo, Tasnim, and Aleck Ostry. *The One Best Way? Breastfeeding History, Politics, and Policy in Canada.* Waterloo, ON: Wilfred Laurier University Press, 2009.

Newell, Felicia D., Patricia L. Williams, and Cynthia G. Watt. "Is the Minimum Enough? Affordability of a Nutritious Diet for Minimum Wage Earners in Nova Scotia (2002–2012)." *Canadian Journal of Public Health* 105, 3 (2014): e158–65.

Newman, Judith M. "Action Research: A Brief Overview." *Forum: Qualitative Social Research* 1, 1 (2000). http://qualitative-research.net/fqs-texte/1-00/1-00newman-e.htm.

Nova Scotia. *Breastfeeding in Nova Scotia: Responsibilities of the Nova Scotia Department of Health and the Nova Scotia Department of Health Promotion and Protection.* Policy statement. Last modified June 2006. https://novascotia.ca/dhw/healthy-communities/documents/Provincial-Breastfeeding-Policy.pdf.

–. *Employment Support and Income Assistance (ESIA) Policy Manual.* 2015. https://novascotia.ca/coms/employment/documents/ESIA_Program_Policy_Manual.pdf.

Ontario. *Ontario Food and Nutrition Strategy: A Comprehensive Evidence Informed Plan for Healthy Food and Food Systems in Ontario.* Ontario Food and Nutrition Strategy Group, 2017.

Orr, Sarah, Naomi Dachner, Lesley Frank, and Valerie Tarasuk. "Relation between Household Food Insecurity and Breastfeeding in Canada." *Canadian Medical Association Journal* 190, 11 (2018): E312–19. https://doi.org/10.1503/cmaj.170880.

Palmer, Gabrielle. *The Politics of Breastfeeding: When Breasts Are Bad for Business.* London: Pandora Press, 2009.

Parent Health Education Resource Working Group. *How to Feed Your Baby with Infant Formula.* Halifax: Nova Scotia Department of Health and Wellness, 2015. https://novascotia.ca.

Park, Kyong, Margaret Kersey, Joni Geppert, Mary Story, Diana Cutts, and John H. Himes. "Household Food Insecurity Is a Risk Factor for Iron-Deficiency Anaemia in a Multi-Ethnic, Low-Income Sample of Infants and Toddlers." *Public Health Nutrition* 12, 11 (2009): 2120–28.

Partyka, Brendine, Susan Whiting, Deanna Grunerud, Karen Archibald, and Kara Quennell. "Infant Nutrition in Saskatoon: Barriers to Infant Food Security." *Canadian Journal of Dietetic Practice and Research* 71, 2 (2010): 79–84.

People's Food Policy Project. *Resetting the Table: A People's Food Policy for Canada.* Montreal: Food Secure Canada, 2011. https://foodsecurecanada.org/sites/foodsecurecanada.org/files/FSC-resetting2012-8half11-lowres-EN.pdf.

Poland, B., K. Frohlich, R.J. Haines, E. Mykhalovskiy, M. Rock, and R. Sparks. "The Social Context of Smoking: The Next Frontier in Tobacco Control?" *Tobacco Control* 15, 1 (2006): 59–63.

Poppendieck, Janet. *Sweet Charity? Emergency Food and the End of Entitlement.* New York: Penguin, 1998.

Power, Elaine M. "Determinants of Healthy Eating among Low-Income Canadians." *Canadian Journal of Public Health* 96, 3 (2005): S37–42.

Public Health Agency of Canada. *The Canada Prenatal Nutrition Program: A Decade of Promoting the Health of Mothers, Babies and Communities.* Ottawa: Minister of Health, 2007.

–. *Protecting, Promoting and Supporting Breastfeeding: A Practical Workbook for Community-Based Programs*. 2nd ed. Ottawa: Public Health Agency of Canada, 2014. http://www.phac-aspc.gc.ca/hp-ps/dca-dea/publications/pdf/ppsb-ppsam-eng.pdf.

Radford, A. *The Ecological Impact of Bottle Feeding*. Report for Baby Milk Action. Cambridge: IBFAN, 1991.

Radimer, Kathy L., Christine M. Olson, Jennifer C. Greene, Cathy C. Campbell, and Jean-Pierre Habicht. "Understanding Hunger and Developing Indicators to Assess It in Women and Children." *Journal of Nutrition Education* 24, 1, supplement 1 (1992): 36S–45S.

Raphael, Dennis, ed. *Social Determinants of Health: Canadian Perspectives*, 3rd ed. Toronto Canadian Scholars' Press, 2016.

Rasmussen, Kathleen M., Julie A. Hilson, and Chris L. Kjolhede. "Obesity May Impair Lactogenesis II." *Journal of Nutrition* 131, 11 (2001): 3009S–11S.

Ricciuto, Laurie, and Valerie S. Tarasuk. "An Examination of Income-Related Disparities in the Nutritional Quality of Food Selections among Canadian Households from 1986–2001." *Social Science and Medicine* 64, 1 (2007): 186–98.

Ricciuto, L., V. Tarasuk, and A. Yatchew. "Socio-Demographic Influences on Food Purchasing among Canadian Households." *European Journal of Clinical Nutrition* 60, 6 (2006): 778–90.

Riches, Graham. *Food Bank Nations: Poverty, Corporate Charity and the Right to Food*. New York: Routledge, 2018.

–. "Food Banks and Food Security: Welfare Reform, Human Rights and Social Policy." *Social Policy and Administration* 36, 6 (2002): 648–63.

–. "Hunger, Food Security and Welfare Policies: Issues and Debates in First World Societies." *Proceedings of the Nutrition Society* 56 (1997): 62–74.

Rideout, Karen, Barbara Seed, and Aleck Ostry. "Putting Food on the Public Health Table: Making Food Security Relevant to Regional Health Authorities." *Canadian Journal of Public Health* 97, 3 (2006): 233–36.

Rose-Jacobs, Ruth, Maureen M. Black, Patrick H. Casey, John T. Cook, Diana B. Cutts, Mariana Chilton, Timothy Heeren, Suzette M. Levenson, Alan F. Meyers, and Deborah A. Frank. "Household Food Insecurity: Associations with At-Risk Infant and Toddler Development." *Pediatrics* 121, 1 (2008): 65–72.

Rosenberg, Kenneth, Carissa A. Eastham, Laurin J. Kasehagen, and Alfredo P. Sandoval. "Marketing Infant Formula through Hospitals: The Impact of Commercial Hospital Discharge Packs on Breastfeeding." *American Journal of Public Health* 98, 2 (2008): 290–95.

Salmon, Libby. "Food Security for Infants and Young Children: An Opportunity for Breastfeeding Policy?" *International Breastfeeding Journal* 10, 7 (2015): n.p. https://doi.org/10.1186/s13006-015-0029-6.

Skalicky, Anne, Alan F. Meyers, William G. Adams, Zhaoyan Yang, John T. Cook, and Deborah A. Frank. "Child Food Insecurity and Iron Deficiency Anemia in Low-Income Infants and Toddlers in the United States." *Maternal and Child Health Journal* 10, 2 (2006): 177–85.

Smith, Paige Hall, Bernice L. Hausman, and Miriam Labbok, eds. *Beyond Health, Beyond Choice: Breastfeeding Constraints and Realities*. New Brunswick, NJ: Rutgers University Press, 2012.

Statistics Canada. *Census in Brief: Children Living in Low-Income Households*. Catalogue no. 98-200-X2016012. Ottawa: Statistics Canada, 2017. http://www12.statcan.gc.ca/census-recensement/2016/as-sa/98-200-x/2016012/98-200-x2016012-eng.cfm.

Strauss, Anselm, and Juliet Corbin. *Basics of Qualitative Research: Grounded Theory Procedures and Techniques,* 4th ed. Newbury Park, CA: Sage, 2014.

Tarasuk, Valerie. *Household and Individual Food Insecurity*. Discussion paper prepared for the Office of Nutrition Policy and Promotion. Ottawa: Health Canada, 2001.

Tarasuk, Valerie, and George H. Beaton. "Household Food Insecurity and Hunger among Families Using Food Banks." *Canadian Journal of Public Health* 90, 2 (1999): 109–13.

Tarasuk, Valerie, and Barbara Davis. "Responses to Food Insecurity in the Changing Canadian Welfare State." *Journal of Nutrition Education* 28, 2 (1996): 71–75.

Tarasuk, Valerie, and Joan M. Eakin. "Charitable Food Assistance as Symbolic Gesture: An Ethnographic Study of Food Banks in Ontario." *Social Science and Medicine* 56, 7 (2003): 1505–15.

Tarasuk, Valerie, and Heather Maclean. "The Food Problems of Low-Income Single Mothers: An Ethnographic Study." *Canadian Home Economics Journal* 40, 2 (1990): 76–82.

Tarasuk, Valerie, Andy Mitchell, and Naomi Dachner. *Household Food Insecurity in Canada, 2014*. Toronto: Research to Identify Policy Option to Reduce Food Insecurity (PROOF), 2016. https://proof.utoronto.ca.

Thomas, W.I. "The Relation of Research to the Social Process." In *W.I. Thomas on Social Organization and Social Personality: Selected Papers,* edited by Morris Janowitz, 289–305. Chicago: University of Chicago Press, 1966.

Townson, Monica, and Kevin Hayes. *Women and the Employment Insurance Program*. Toronto: Canadian Centre for Policy Alternatives, 2007. http://www.policyalternatives.ca.

Travers, Kim D. "The Social Organization of Nutritional Inequities." *Social Science and Medicine* 43, 4 (1996): 543–53.

United Nations Children's Fund (UNICEF). *Innocenti Declaration: On the Protection, Promotion and Support of Breastfeeding*. WHO/UNICEF Policymakers' Meeting,

Florence, July 30–August 1, 1990. http://www.unicef.org/programme/breastfeeding/innocenti.htm.

–. *Innocenti Declaration 2005: On Infant and Young Child Feeding*. Adopted at "Celebrating Innocenti 1990–2005: Achievements, Challenges and Future Imperatives," Florence, November 22, 2005. http://innocenti15.net/declaration.pdf.pdf.

United Nations Office of the High Commissioner for Human Rights. *CESCR General Comment No. 12: The Right to Adequate Food (Art. 11)*. Adopted at the 20th session of the Committee on Economic, Social and Cultural Rights, May 12, 1999. https://www.refworld.org/pdfid/4538838c11.pdf.

–. *Convention on the Rights of the Child*. Adopted by General Assembly Resolution 44/25, November 20, 1989. https://www.ohchr.org/en/professionalinterest/pages/crc.aspx.

–. *International Covenant on Economic, Social and Cultural Rights*. Adopted by General Assembly Resolution 2200A (XXI), December 16, 1966. https://www.ohchr.org/en/professionalinterest/pages/cescr.aspx.

–. *Universal Declaration of Human Rights*. Adopted by General Assembly Resolution 217A, December 10, 1948. https://undocs.org/A/RES/217(III).

Van Esterik, Penny. *Beyond the Breast-Bottle Controversy*. New Brunswick, NJ: Rutgers University Press, 1989.

–. "Right to Food, Right to Feed, Right to be Fed: The Intersection of Women's Rights and the Right to Food." *Agriculture and Human Values* 16, 2 (1999): 225–32.

Voices for Food Security in Nova Scotia. *Can Nova Scotians Afford to Eat Healthy? Report on 2015 Participatory Food Costing*. Halifax: Food Action Research Centre (FoodARC), Mount Saint Vincent University, 2017. https://foodarc.ca.

Vozoris, Nicholas, Barbara Davis, and Valerie Tarasuk. "The Affordability of a Nutritious Diet for Households on Welfare in Toronto." *Canadian Journal of Public Health* 93, 1 (2002): 36–40.

Vozoris, Nicholas T., and Valerie S. Tarasuk. "Household Food Insufficiency Is Associated with Poorer Health." *Journal of Nutrition* 133, 1 (2003): 120–26.

Wallace, Lora Ebert, and Holly Chason. "Infant Feeding in the Modern World: Medicalization and the Maternal Body." *Sociological Spectrum* 27, 4 (2007): 405–38.

Warde, Alan. *The Practice of Eating*. Cambridge: Polity Press, 2016.

Weir, Erica. "Powdered Infant Formula and Fatal Infection with *Enterobacter sakazakii*." *Canadian Medical Association Journal* 166, 12 (2002): 1570.

Williams, Patricia L., Christine P. Johnson, Meredith L.V. Kratzmann, C. Shanthi Jacob Johnson, Barbara J. Anderson, and Cathy Chenhall. "Can Households Earning Minimum Wage in Nova Scotia Afford a Nutritious Diet?" *Canadian Journal of Public Health* 97, 6 (2006): 430–34.

Williams, Patricia L., Rita B. MacAulay, Barbara J. Anderson, Kimberlee Barro, Doris E. Gillis, Christine P. Johnson, Lynn L. Langille, Shelley Moran, and Debra E. Reimer. "'I Would Have Never Thought That I Would Be in Such a Predicament': Voices from Women Experiencing Food Insecurity in Nova Scotia, Canada." *Journal of Hunger and Environmental Nutrition* 7, 2–3 (2012): 253–70.

Williams, Patricia L., Cynthia G. Watt, Michelle Amero, Barbara J. Anderson, Ilya Blum, Rebecca Green-LaPierre, Christine P. Johnson, and Debra E. Reimer. "Affordability of a Nutritious Diet for Income Assistance Recipients in Nova Scotia (2002–2010)." *Canadian Journal of Public Health* 103, 3 (2012): 183–88.

Willis, Claire Elizabeth, and Verity Livingstone. "Infant Insufficient Milk Syndrome Associated with Maternal Postpartum Hemorrhage." *Journal of Human Lactation* 11, 2 (1995): 123–26.

World Health Organization (WHO). *International Code of Marketing of Breast-Milk Substitutes.* Geneva: WHO, 1981. http://www.who.int/nutrition/publications/code_english.pdf.

Yin, Robert K. *Case Study Research: Design and Methods,* 5th ed. Thousand Oaks, CA: Sage Publications, 2014.

Zaslow, Martha, Jacinta Bronte-Tinkew, Randolph Capps, Allison Horowitz, Kristin Moore, and Debra Weinstein. "Food Security during Infancy: Implications for Attachment and Mental Proficiency in Toddlerhood." *Maternal and Child Health Journal* 13, 1 (2009): 66–80.

Index

Note: "(f)" after a page number indicates a figure.